C000099752

*For Hakim and Shoshana
and for all who have taught me
the urgency of liberating pastoral supervision
from its colonial Christian history.*

*We are at our best when the table is long,
all voices are valued, and we stay curious
as both teachers and learners.*

Brené Brown

Work is the place
where the self meets the world.

David Whyte, Poet[1]

Supervision is an invitation to 'live your soul'
and reconnect with the 'passion [that] arises
when the essence of one's life has been touched
and one starts dealing with the world from that
place.

Jochen Encke, Psychotherapist.[2]

Supervision is a way of reconnecting with that
rage of the heart that gets us up every day to
practice our helping and healing arts.

Sheila Ryan, Homeopath[3]

Note to the reader

The material here was created for the ear, not for the eye. Its genesis lies in talks, conference presentations and professional development workshops given between 2018 – 2020 in Australia, Malta, Scotland, Ireland and England. What you will read lacks the dynamism of the live moment, the attentiveness of the original audiences, their delight and (not infrequently) their discomfort, their interjections, questions and raucous laughter. I am indebted to those who offered me critical friendship in revising my thinking and improving the material. And to you who are about to hear this for the first time I encourage you to follow the advice of Bruce Lee: 'Absorb what is helpful, discard what is useless and add what is uniquely your own'.

Foreword

From the deck of a cruise ship traversing the Norwegian Fjords I saw the image on the front cover of this book. Suspended hundreds of metres above the Fjord, it depicts a small rock wedged between two large rock faces: one bathed in light, one veiled in shadow. The sight was mesmerising. 'That's me, that's me' cried a voice inside. 'That's me, caught between a rock and a hard place dangling in mid-air. That's me trapped between light and shadow.' But if at first viewing, what I saw spoke of precarious vulnerability, the longer I looked the more I recognised that the middle rock was being held in precise, balanced tension by the rocks on either side; wedged but not abandoned; held but not dropped.

As a priest, psychotherapist, supervisor and adult educator, I have spent much of my life being formed, re-formed and (thankfully) transformed for my professional task. I have been privileged to have had a wonderful academic and professional formation. I have sat at the feet of masters and been coached and mentored by leaders in their fields. But now, as I begin to pass the baton to the next generation, I find myself between a rock and a hard place in which the traditions which formed me, the professional wisdom I have imbibed and the dominant paradigms and frames of reference which govern my life's work, no longer hold me, no longer support me and no longer shape my true identity.[4] 'Keep your distance' says professional wisdom; 'bridge the gap' I reply. 'Have firm boundaries' I was taught; 'get up close and personal' I insist. 'Insure yourself against your clients' I was advised; 'build relationships from love' I teach.

Caught between a rock and a hard place, I have mostly kept my own counsel. But increasingly, in recent years, I have found myself supporting people who also feel dangled in the air, suspended between the worlds of regulatory control, scrutiny and governance (the shadow) and the, as yet under explored worlds of humane and compassionate praxis (the light). Occupying that liminal space between the familiarities of the past and the uncertainties of the future demands courage, companionship and commitment. Professional wisdom admonishes me to stick to the old-and-tried ways and the securities they offer. After all, it would be professional suicide to step out of line. And who in their right mind would throw away their career in a moment of madness? But 'Go!', says my inner spirit, 'you have a calling' and 'only you can bring forth your potential.'[5]

This book is for professional trespassers, boundary crossers and migrants. It is for people who love questions more than answers. And it is for professional magpies and scavengers who prefer the pursuit of wisdom to the acquisition of knowledge. If that is you, then consider yourself invited to share this space between a rock and a hard place with me as we shelter each other from the wind and the rain and rest in the assurance that 'the soul is tough, resilient and resourceful: it knows how to survive in hard places.'[6]

Pastoral Supervision

Chapter One
What's in a word?

Words slip, slide, decay with imprecision,
will not stay in place, will not stay still.

T S Eliot[7]

Few words carry as much baggage or press as many buttons from practitioners across the professions as the word 'supervision'. The negative connotations which link it with institutional surveillance and big brother watching over your shoulder has led some to call it *snooper*-vision. And yet the etymology of the word suggests something much more dynamic and rewarding.

In Latin, *super* denotes over or above and *videre* (the verb from which we get the English word *vision*) means to see. Putting those two words together gives us *over*-seeing; a view from above; a bigger picture; a broader horizon or a panoramic perspective. Supervision is all about vision and, at its best, the supervisory encounter is the meeting point of visionaries: people who have been captured by a vision of their role in the world, of how life can be and of how best to express their care for others.

And yet, paradoxically, the very promotion of supervision as standard practice in professional lives poses the greatest threat to participants experiencing it as either visionary or super. Like many, over my career I have been subjected to *mini* vision, the bargain option in which supervisors limit what is explored in the session to some small confining area rather than to the *super* or expansive view which I have been seeking. At other times

I have been offered *tunnel vision* when my supervisors have been so intent on pursuing their own agendas that I have withered and shrunk rather than expanded in their presence.

The explosion of supervision across the professions, led largely by quality control measures which increasingly govern professional practice, simultaneously 'strengthen the mandate' for supervision and threaten its integrity as a 'worker-centred and a learning-focused activity.'[8] As a result supervision often

> 'veers between line management aimed at compliance with procedures and checklists and safe surface exploration. This type of supervision becomes mundane with a 'must do' rather than 'want to do' energy and does not take up the learning opportunities that are possible. The investment in the relationship becomes perfunctory and tends to be corrective rather than transformative'.[9]

No wonder supervision has such a bad press when it is being sabotaged by supervisors who trade in managerial compliance rather than in soulful vision. For what is *super* about having someone checking up on you to make sure there are no oversights? What is *super* about having someone analyse or diagnose your professional practice only to prescribe treatment plans that you are meant to follow? And what is *visionary* about being held hostage for an hour while the person in the other chair gets their ego needs met by showing off their wisdom and experience.

My first experience of supervision was as a trainee counsellor being supervised by someone within the training organisation. With no choice over who would supervise me, my initiation into supervision was with a person I neither liked nor warmed to. For three years I was poked and prodded, tried and tested as if I was an avocado on the supermarket shelf, uncertain whether I would be picked or discarded. I don't think for a minute that is what my supervisor intended – I honestly believe she wanted to bring out the very best in me – but that's how those weekly sessions felt to me. What she called 'supervision', I called 'death by inquisition'. The experience was perfunctory. I performed for her, learned what lines to deliver and - even more importantly - what lines to hold back. More than anything I played the game. I learned little about practice, but a great deal about survival.

Thirty years on, I spend my life sitting with people, individually and in groups, some of whom come willingly, some because they have been sent, some because they need to comply with professional expectations. Those who come willingly are a joy to be with. Their curiosity, their struggles to find meaning in complexity, and their commitment to telling the truth about their professional lives touches me deeply. Such reflexive living is underpinned by three commitments

- to reflect on the past in the present for the sake of the future
- to turn experience into an opportunity for learning
- to enhance their ability to reflect-*in*-action (in real time) through the habit of reflection-*on*-action (after the event).[10]

I never fail to be inspired by such wholehearted practitioners and feel humbled and honoured in their presence. Their embodied witness fuels my courage and determination and ability to be the best I can as a supervisor.

In contrast, those who come to supervision, out of a sense of duty or simply because they 'have to' have the opposite effect on me. Time drags. Sessions lack energy. Maintaining the status quo is the name of the game, not transformation or the pursuit of insight. Such supervisees typically resort to reporting (narrating what is going on) rather than to reflecting (searching for the meaning in what is going on). They risk nothing. They lose nothing. They find nothing. And while low risk taking is to be expected at the early stages of a supervisory relationship, when it becomes the norm, 'deeper learning' and transformative potential are 'left outside the door'.[11]

The Australian poet Noel Davis could have had transformative supervision in mind when he wrote these lines:

Venture beyond the familiar.
Range wider than routine.
Delve beneath the certain.
Hold truth with an open heart.
Break from the programmed
whatever it be.
Take a different way home.[12]

How different that is from what so often happens in supervision when the unwritten contract seems more akin to

Do what you have always done.
Repeat the tried and the tested.
Risk nothing, learn nothing.
Fake it and get through.
Give in to the same old,
same old uncritically.
Go home on autopilot.[13]

Having had more than my share of supervisors and supervisees who have settled for repeating the tried and the tested I have come to recognise three rewards which arise when we risk 'venturing beyond the familiar' and 'delving beneath the certain'.

Reward One - We are not alone
The first pay back for *engaging* in supervision (as opposed to simply *attending* sessions) is the discovery that we are not alone and that others also stumble and stutter, feel unsure or inadequate, become overwhelmed or find themselves completely at sea in their practices. Admitting those things in supervision reinforces the truth that we are in it together. The sheer relief of telling the truth about our practice rather than hiding behind our intricate professional barricades releases us from living in isolation and restores a sense of belonging to a community of flawed yet faithful practice. In so doing we recognise each other not just as human *resources* but as human beings. And while it is true that *informational* learning can happen in solitude, *transformational* learning requires relationship.

'What arises through this relationship becomes the vehicle for changing how we understand ourselves and each other. The quality of relationship is what allows us to feel safe enough to trust, to take emotional risks, to allow ourselves to be seen in our uncertainty and vulnerability, to uncover the biases and beliefs that we unconsciously use to construct our identities and ways of knowing and to see ourselves and others from fresh perspectives'. [14]

Reward Two – Risks pay off

There is much truth in the saying 'if you always do what you have always done, you will always find what you have always found'. In my experience, supervision becomes transformative when it 'interrupts practice', 'disturbs stuck narratives' and 'wakes us up to what we are doing' for 'when we are alive to what we are doing, we wake up to what is, instead of falling asleep in the comfort stories of our routines and daily practice' (Ryan 2004:47). Transformative reflection invites us into the centre of our own doubts only to be met there, not by the wagging finger of condemnation, but by the respectful curiosity of wondering 'what if?' (Ryan 2004:22) Those who choose to limit their supervisory repertoire to simply reporting what they have been doing rather than enquiring as to its meaning or delving deeper into the contextual dynamics in which their work is set will never know the rewards that come from risking deeper engagement and trust.

Reward Three - Care for the carer

Much professional life takes place in 'noisy, public and stressful environments'.[15] Conversations with colleagues are often interrupted, hurried and task or information based. Supervision becomes transformative when we 'allow, albeit briefly, the doors to shut, the noise to be reduced and a quiet space for satisfying professional conversation'.[16] In that protected and safe place, the rejected stone of self-care may indeed become the cornerstone that can sustain us, recharge us and propel us back into the world to face the demands of life at the frontline of practice.

And so while some see supervision as yet one more box to tick to fend off managerial scrutiny I remain committed to the bigger picture which has the potential to go beyond meeting the *normative* needs of organizations and institutions to not only include attending to the *restorative* needs of practitioners (to offload, find support and draw breath to face another day) but to also foster the *transformative* potential of supervision in helping workers reconnect with the vision – the soulful, motivating heartbeat that brought them into the caring profession in the first place. For when someone reconnects with their lifegiving purpose, then performance is inevitably improved and job satisfaction inevitably enriched.

For Reflection

1. In what ways could the supervision you engage in be termed *super* and *visionary*?

2. To what extent does the supervision you engage in 'venture beyond the familiar, range wider than routine and delve beneath the certain?'

3. In what ways does the supervision you offer or receive 'repeat the tried and the tested and give in to the same old, same old'?

4. What would it take for supervision to become not only normative but transformative for you?

Chapter Two
Evolving Understandings

Pastoral supervision as a distinctive form of professional supervision is an emerging discipline. As such it is in its infancy with a very limited bibliography.[17] The UK *Association for Pastoral Supervision and Education* (APSE) was only founded in 2009 and its Australian counterpart *Transforming Practices* in 2007 As a result, what many people understand by pastoral supervision is simply the supervision *of* pastoral work. Not surprising then that until fairly recently, adaptation and translation from the worlds of therapeutic or social work supervision have dominated the field with many supervisors operating out of a therapeutic than a pastoral paradigm. Even more disconcerting is the narrowing of the equation which understands pastoral as pertaining to the realm of faith groups and the practise of ministers of religion.

In an attempt to reclaim the distinctiveness of the emerging discipline of pastoral supervision I attempted this definition in 2016.

> Pastoral Supervision is a safe, boundaried and hospitable space in which people with a duty of care reflect on their use of time, talents and roles in their work with others. It pays attention to the worker as well as the work is truthful about the past, attentive to the present and directed towards a transformative future.[18]

What I was trying to do in that short statement was three things.

- to release 'pastoral' from its exclusive faith context;

- to revision 'pastoral' as an ethical or attitudinal stance in which pastoral describes a way of holding the other (the supervisee *and* those on the receiving end of the supervisee's care) with care, compassion and commitment;
- to highlight the attention paid to a person's underlying motivation or vocation as the distinguishing hallmark of pastoral supervision.

Frederick Buechner defines vocation as 'the place where our deep gladness and the world's deep hunger meet.' And that to me is a matter for pastoral supervision. Because while I firmly believe that vocation, the underlying motivational force that first brought us into nursing, social work, teaching etc is a deeply personal matter, I equally believe that it is anything but private.

To put it bluntly: our vocations are *public* property not *private* property. Each of us has a task to perform for the wellbeing of society and it is that conversation - about how we are faring in spending ourselves in the service of others - that lies at the heart of pastoral supervision. So, for example, when a nurse opts for pastoral (as distinct from clinical) supervision, the material she brings to the session is underpinned at a deeper level by an ongoing sustained conversation about

- her stewarding of her nursing gift
- areas where her practice is congruent with her underlying motivation and where is it dissonant?
- and what she wants to do about the gaps between her best aspirations and her actual practice?

Rarely is the vocational conversation as explicit as I have outlined but as soon as I – as supervisor - ask 'how does the story you are telling me today sit with your personal values?' then the conversation we are having in supervision has the word 'vocation' written all over it.

Soul, Role and Context
If my 2016 attempt to define pastoral supervision was the fruit of sweat and toil my next attempt came with no effort whatsoever on my part on a train journey to work in March 2018. Four minutes into my journey a woman got on and took a seat across from me. On the table between us she plonked down a rucksack which bore the message 'Inspiring people to care about the planet'; she then peeled off her coat to reveal a T shirt which said: 'On Wednesdays we smash patriarchy'; and then proceeded to extract from her rucksack a bright orange book with the title: 'The subtle art of not giving a F*ck.[19]

What a morning! What a message! She was clearly someone who stood for something, someone who had no shortage of convictions and someone who had no hesitation in letting the world know about them. And there she was sitting opposite *me,* a priest in civvies, giving nothing away about my convictions, except that I shopped at North Face, Levis and George at Asda.

I was fascinated by the woman and wanted to engage her in conversation. But it was a Wednesday! And I was a man! And I wasn't up for being smashed! I wanted to know the story behind the T shirt and whether she was on her way to a political demo or just wore clothes like this to her work everyday? I wanted to know whether she had a T shirt for all the other days of the week and if she did what did the one for Sunday say. And what about the book – did she really 'not give a F*ck' or, as I suspected, was she a woman who cared deeply about a number of things (which is what that book is actually about)?

As I sat there, in awe of what was unfolding before me, I could hear my mother's voice telling me not to stare – which was, of course, exactly what I was doing. I certainly didn't want to get caught staring at a woman's chest on a train. And so I took out my phone to do what I *normally* do when travelling and opened the biblical App to read the scripture passage allotted to the day only to find these lines from Deuteronomy 4:

> Take care and be earnestly on your guard not to forget the things which your eyes have seen, nor let them slip from your memory as long as you live, but teach them to your children and to your children's children.

Really – The rucksack? The T Shirt? The book title? What an invitation! Reflecting on that train journey helped me understand something that I had been struggling to articulate for many, many years and it is this

Pastoral Supervision is the intentional dialogue between Soul, Role and Context.

Soul
By soul I mean

- that deep underlying motivation in a person's work
- what takes them tick
- what gets them out of bed in the morning

- the fire in their belly that provides meaning and purpose
- the impulse to contribute something to the common good

And so I think of

- a nurse driven by a deep sense of care and compassion
- a social worker committed to righting the wrongs inflicted upon looked after children
- A therapist who wants to help others find freedom
- a teacher who believes in her students potential

'Ask what makes you come alive and go do it' says Howard Thurman 'because what the world needs is people who have come alive.' That's the kind of soulful living I am talking about when people find a way to live out their motivating purpose in their working lives. And what I have learned as a supervisor over the years is that when people have the opportunity to do the kind of soulful work that helps them come alive, the kind of work that is worth getting out of bed in the morning for, then although they get tired, generally speaking, their work energises and refuels them. Conversely, when people become estranged or divorced from their life-giving purpose, or neglect to attend to what matters most to them, then their energy dissipates and job satisfaction diminishes. And 'when your soul is tired, no amount of sleep will restore you.'[20]

That lady on the train had bucket loads of soul and was certainly highly motivated. She certainly wasn't short of reasons to get out of bed in the morning. She had a very strong sense of vocation and was upfront and unashamed about it. But it's one thing to tell a crowd of commuters what you stand for and what you really think but it is quite another thing to live out those beliefs when you get to work? And that is where role comes in.

Role

I am using 'role' as shorthand for the job or post a person holds; the thing - paid or voluntary - to which they give their time, effort and attention. Some roles offer the Cinderella factor: the shoe fits and the job provides the opportunity to express the very things that matter most to us. So for example, someone who has a real passion for working with children (soul) and is fortunate enough to get a position which allows them to express that, is likely to find their soul and roles aligned and to experience joy at work. Whereas, if the only post available to a person whose soul is drawn to children's work is with older people with dementia, then the dissonance between soul and role is likely to be intensified and demand some careful negotiation.

Being soulfully motivated is one thing but roles limit as well as enable and professional roles release as well as restrain. For every person for whom a change in role – a change in post – marks a recalibration of the soul in the direction of self-fulfilment, countless others who went into a profession alive, awake and alert have stories to tell about souls that shrivelled and withered in the roles they inhabited.

I think of people whose souls were ablaze in one role but whose inner pilot light went out in another. I think of vocational teachers who buckle under the weight of data protection, health and safety, the demands of safeguarding or continuous scrutiny and inspection. I think of counsellors torn down the middle between their personal and instinctive responses to clients' issues and the restrictions that time limited working practices and regulatory bodies place upon them. And saddest of all, I think of practitioners who sold their souls to pursue some coveted role only to find it failed to deliver the personal and professional satisfaction that it promised.

If the lady on the train worked in a women's refuge or in an organisation campaigning for social change then, the chances are, when she gets off the train and arrives at work, her inner and outer worlds, her soul and her role might well be harmoniously aligned. But just imagine what would happen if her role – the job she held – was in some capitalist, 'jobs for the boys' sort of business conglomerate where her personal values were diametrically opposed to the values of the company. I wonder then how she would manage the tug of war between what her soul held dear and what the day job demanded of her and on which her livelihood depends? And it is that tug of war between the desires of the soul and demands of the role that I see day in day out as I support staff in supervision.

Context
So far, I have outlined the relationship between soul and role in personal and professional wellbeing. But context has a crucial role to play in determining whether a person's soul and role can come together in harmony or be wedged apart. By context I mean the nitty gritty realities that go far beyond the obvious matching of temperament, likes and dislikes to posts available. By

context I mean organisational cultures, values and behaviours, ethos and atmospheres, management styles and work practices. Attending to context in supervision asks whether the working environment is characterised by the presence or absence of trust? Are staff encouraged or hindered from exercising autonomy? Are relationships healthy or toxic?

A person who secures their dream job only to discover a few days into the new post that staff relationships are strained, that there is a prevailing culture of bullying which goes unchallenged or that everyone is watching their back, is unlikely to experience wellbeing and joy at work no matter how aligned their soul and role may be. Context more than anything explains why people whose souls and roles were in harmony in one appointment become utterly discordant in another.

Speaking personally, I have been a chaplain in three different hospices over my career. In the first and second I flourished. My role enabled me to express my soul in supportive and inspirational contexts. But in the third, I withered. And not because I lost my soul or vocation for the work. I didn't. Nor because I could no longer inhabit the role and its demands. I withered quite simply because the context was so dysfunctional and the relationships between management and frontline staff so toxic that it felt as if the hospice itself had terminal agitation and that none of the painkillers available to us could get on top of it. In the space of three years that hospice lost some of its most experienced, wholehearted soulful practitioners. As chaplain to that unit, powerless to stop the contextual tsunami, I withered.

Circles of Wellbeing
I have already outlined the first lesson the nameless woman on the train taught me namely that pastoral supervision fosters the intentional dialogue between soul, role and context.

The second thing that encounter taught me was that pastoral supervision attends to three concentric circles of wellbeing:

- Inner wellbeing:
  living in harmony with your soul and personal value systems

- Professional wellbeing:
  being able to inhabit and discharge the expectations of the role

- Contextual wellbeing:
  Attending to the health of organisations, systems, communities of practice and professions.

Between a rock and a hard place
Twenty years ago when I first began to supervise, people came more often than not because they had lost touch with their soul or life-giving purpose. Nowadays what I see, day in day out, are much more nuanced symptoms of vocational wounding[21] which arise not so much from a loss of heart or soul for the work as from the struggle to find ways of expressing or reconciling soul with the demands of role and the particularities of context.

Joseph Sittler, an American pastor, speaks for many a practitioner struggling to bring soul, role and context into harmonious dialogue when he writes about the 'maceration of the minister' sitting in his study surrounded by books from college days gathering dust, on top of which are piled architects plans, letters from the bank, tile samples and a plumber's estimate. He concludes 'and so the prophet becomes an entrepreneur and ministers who are ordained to an office too often end up running an office.'[22] It is indeed wonderful when a practitioner can find a way to bring all three dimensions – soul, role and context - together but it is more common to struggle with at least one of those dimensions at any given time in our professional lives.

When up against it, those who default to soul (to the detriment of role and context) often act out of a privatised sense of purpose and motivation. They fly solo and do their own thing. And while they are happy to take a wage from their employers, (or to be allowed to operate as a volunteer in a given agency) the views and needs of the organisation they work for do not really figure in their self-understanding. Not surprisingly, when soul-priority folk come to supervision, they often present with tales of woe about not being allowed to do what they really want to do and of how their bosses simply don't understand them. Supervisors should beware of colluding with such privatised and a-contextual narratives.

Unable to bring soul, role and context into harmony leads others to default to role and to simply get the job done no matter the cost to themselves. Role-based folks, are usually diligent, reliable and dutiful and are often rewarded for their hard work with promotion. However, scratch the surface and you will often find a dissonance between their inner selves (soul) and their outer selves (role). They smile on the outside while, unknown to others, groan in the inside. And unless role-based practitioners can find ways to bring their soul's motivation into conversation with the job they do, they are unlikely to feel fulfilled and professionally satisfied.

In my experience role-based supervisees tend towards one of two things. They either *over* work in the day job in the hope that somehow, some day, their soul's joy will return or they accept the day job for what it is and then compensate for the lack of fulfilment it brings by taking on additional responsibilities elsewhere (pursuing a course; joining a committee; becoming involved in some non-work related project) which speaks to their soul's unmet needs.

Soul, Role and Context in practice
In practical terms, supervision which intentionally fosters dialogue between soul, role and context invites courageous conversation by asking

- How do your soul and role fare at work?
- When did your soul and role last come together in the workplace?
- When, at work, do you find yourself acting from the deep values by which you live?
- And when, in your work, are your soul and role not talking to each other or estranged?
- How does your context inhibit or release you for others?

Admittedly it takes courage and trust to have conversations of this kind which go far deeper than traditional forms of supervision envisage, but the transformative benefits of seeing workers reconnect their inner motivation with their actual practice within their given context is invaluable.

For Reflection

1. How do your soul and role fare at work?

2. When did soul and role last come together in the workplace?

3. When, at work, do you find yourself acting from the deep values by which you live?

4. And when, in your work, are your soul and role not talking to each other or estranged?

5. How does your context inhibit or release you for others?

Chapter Three
A changing conversation

'Supervision is a changing conversation' writes Joan Wilmot and how true that is. [23] We know from experience that supervision – *as a practice* – is a conversation which changes perspectives and indeed changes lives. But we also know that supervision - *as a discipline* – is an ever-changing conversation. In an attempt to capture and distil what has been happening in print and in professional dialogues over the past twenty years since Kenneth Pohly first coined the term 'pastoral supervision' in 1977[24] I have chosen to ground this book within the supervisory space itself by offering a verbatim account of the first five minutes of an actual supervision session in which I was the supervisor and Fiona was the supervisee. I do this intentionally because what you the reader make of the story you are about to hear and where your thoughts take you immediately, raises questions about

- how you understand pastoral supervision
- the lenses or filters through which you hear material in supervision
- and the modalities you use to explore what people bring to supervision.

As you read, I invite you to

- put yourself in the shoes of the supervisor
- identify what you consider to be the core issue(s)
- and ponder how you might help the supervisee explore that issue in the remaining 55 minutes of the session.

Supervision Scenario

Fiona arrived on time as usual.
A loyal sort, she never misses her appointments.
But between *her* knocking and *me* opening
I saw her through the window
parking and getting out of her car.

Everything about her looked weary
as if the world was on her shoulders.
30 seconds was all it took for me to clock it.
And 30 seconds was all she needed
to do what she had done so many times over the years:
rearrange her face, erase her frown lines
and put on her cheery professional mask.

Normally she could do that in five seconds.
Even sooner if she saw someone she knew in the supermarket
but today she barely managed her own transfiguration in 30.

'Welcome', I said, 'the kettle's on.'
And while I withdrew to the kitchen,
awaiting the familiar whistle from the gas stove,
I wondered what Fiona had brought
and whether she would leave still carrying it
or if, in our time together, I could help her lay it down.

Fiona knew about eliciting a focus
and as always came prepared.

'My team got a rave review from the Care Inspectorate'
she smarted, 'But I feel dead inside.'

No messing around here, I noticed.
No small chat or warm up.

We were straight in.
The session had started.

'I saw it as you arrived' I said,
And then wondered if I should have stayed silent.

For a minute or so neither of us spoke ....
The clock ticked ....

'The build up was such a slog' she continued.
'but I'm used to hard work and I just got on with it.

I can *do* hard work.
But this whole 'celebrate your success' malarkey
that's a whole different ball game.'

.... *more silence* ...

'Is that what you want to focus on today?' I asked gingerly,
(anxious not to miss the point
but even more anxious of focusing in too soon.)

'Its not that I don't think getting 6 out of 6 is good'
she said, looking at me for reassurance
'its just that I feel empty and numb.'

'I put on a party for the staff and really got into it.
I stayed late one night
and decorated the staff room with bunting and balloons.
The place looked fabulous
But I felt nothing.'

'I gave a wee speech
and told them all how proud I was
of what he had all achieved.'

I caught the crack in her voice
and saw her eyes fill up.

'And I totally meant it.
I told them how much they had pulled together
and how rare it was for the Inspectors to give out 6s.
I was all bubbly on the outside but inside I felt empty.
It was weird.It was like being in it
and being a fly on the wall watching it at the same time.
I felt such a fake.

But once the day staff had gone home
and the night shift had gone back to their duties
I felt as if I had thrown
all sense of achievement in the bin
with the paper plates and
the dried up sausage rolls.

Running out of words
she stared intently at the carpet.

I too had nothing to say
but the parallel process hadn't escaped me.

The story she was telling
about tears and bin bags
was being replayed
right here, right now between us.
It was a while since I had felt
any sense of professional achievement
no matter how much people affirmed me.
Like Fiona,
there was a gap between
my insides and my outsides.

'What happened then?'
I asked, risking breaking the silence.

'Oh, I dried my eyes, put on my mask
and went home wondering if I would ever come back.'

'Wow', I said, 'wow!'

more silence

'Yep I was completely washed out.
I had spent the evening whipping up a party
but I spent that night utterly defeated, curled up on the sofa.'

'I'm worn out by trying so hard.
This job is killing me.
No one told me it would be like this.
I want my life back.'[25]

For Reflection

1. What do you consider to be the core issue(s) that Fiona (the supervisee) is bringing to supervision?

2. How could you (as supervisor) help Fiona explore that issue in the remaining 55 minutes of the supervision session?

Chapter Four
Frames and Lenses[26]

'The meaning that any event has, depends upon the 'frame' in which we perceive it. When we change the frame, we change the meaning. When the meaning changes, the person's responses and behaviours also change.' [27]

What Bandler and Grindler are saying is very apposite, because Fiona could have taken that story you have just read to personal counselling, to life coaching or to line management each of which would have perceived her story through a different frame and made meaning according to its own particular focus.

But she didn't. Fiona took that story to a room which said 'pastoral supervision' on the door and to someone with whom she has a contract for that purpose and that purpose only. Now as it happens, as Fiona's supervisor, I am *also* a counsellor and someone who (in another setting) has managerial responsibility. But had I stepped out of my supervisory role to play the counselling or work consultancy card, I would have dented Fiona's trust, abdicated my supervisory role and breached our contract. Why? Because 'when we change the frame, we change the meaning. And when the meaning changes, then the speaker and the listener's responses and behaviours change too.' [28]

'The lens we look through will determine what we see.''[29]

In this chapter I want to briefly outline five supervisory lenses through which Fiona's story could be seen. Each of which re-visions the role of the supervisor and locates, dislocates and relocates the expertise he or she requires.

The Diagnostic Lens: What's going on?
Supervising through a diagnostic lens requires the supervisor to have the expertise to diagnose what the supervisee's core issues actually are and then to begin to prescribe and dispense accordingly. Diagnostic supervision can be invaluable especially when supervisees find themselves feeling professionally stuck. Nevertheless, the diagnostic lens needs to be employed with caution lest it unleash a wild goose chase in which the supervisor's fascination takes over and the supervisee becomes disengaged.

In the scenario you have just read, I certainly listened carefully to what Fiona was telling me, but I would have been fundamentally mistaken if I had presumed to have known either the *meaning* of what Fiona was bringing or her *intentions* in bringing it. Supervisors who are drawn to the diagnostic lens need to rein in their desire for analysis until they have asked the supervisee the most important question of all which is:

- what are you looking for in bringing that story to supervision today? *or*
- what are you hoping for in telling me that story?

Such questions and their derivatives do four things

1. They make the supervisee and not the supervisor centre stage;
2. They remind both parties that this space is for supervision and no other purpose;

3. They foster the supervisee's ownership of the session;
4. And they ask the supervisee to direct and focus the supervisor's curiosity and not the other way round.

This is crucial because without that focus, supervisors are likely to start exploring whatever interests them rather than asking supervisees to scratch where the itch is. And after all whose session is it? The supervisor's? Or the supervisee's?

The Solution Lens: How can this be fixed?
One of the things that can easily happen when supervisors *assume* rather than check what supervisees hope to gain when they present material for supervision (especially if the material is complex and emotionally taxing for the supervisee), is that they start chasing solutions. And when that happens the key question becomes: 'What would it take to fix this?' How that question is put depends on skill and experience. Overly responsible supervisors ask: 'How can I solve this *for* you?' Whereas those who are keen to foster supervisees' autonomy ask: 'How can I help you solve this *for yourself?*' Either way, when supervision sees through a solving lens, problems rather than persons take centre stage and finding remedies rather than exploring what is really going on takes over.

Supervisors often get caught in the trap of wanting to fix things for others quite simply because they are deeply caring people who hate to see others in pain. But the clue lies in the name we have chosen for our profession: *pastoral* supervision not *palliative* supervision. Palliative care tries to take pain away. Pastoral care does the opposite. It refuses to dispense pain killers and accompanies people further into their pain until its power and energy is exhausted. What Brené Brown says of faith could equally be said of supervision.

'I thought faith would say: 'I'll take away the pain and the discomfort. But what it ended up saying was 'I'll sit with you in it'.

In my experience supervisees don't need someone to 'take away their pain and discomfort' so much as they need to hear supervisors say: 'I'll sit with you in it'. And that is a much slower and costlier business altogether.[30]

In summary, the plus side of solution focused supervision is that it can take the heat out of the moment and give supervisees a sense that their plight is being taken seriously. But the downside is that it can turn supervision into something transactional rather than relational and leave supervisees feeling diminished. For those reasons, I am not inclined to support supervision through a solution focused lens without the twin guarantees that a) this is what the supervisee is looking for and b) the route to identifying a solution is supervisee (rather than supervisor) led.

The Interpretative Lens: What does it really mean?
Moving along the axis from managerial or therapeutic forms of supervision towards a more transformative and *super*-visionary pastoral paradigm, supervising through an interpretative lens goes 'behind the scenes' and 'beneath the words' of the material being explored. And so if solution focused supervision asks 'what needs

fixing?', interpretative or hermeneutical supervision asks 'what's the story behind the story?' with its corollary questions:

- who are the actors and what part do they play?
- who has a voice and who doesn't?'
- who has power and who doesn't?
- and what hidden factors and dynamics are at work here?[31]

And so if we were to explore the material Fiona brought in the supervision scenario through an interpretive lens we might try to understand the disharmony in her soul, role and context by

- enquiring whether her workload in the weeks leading up to the Inspection might have exacerbated things for her
- or by seeking to delve under her words and ask whether her 'weariness' actually stems from work or from other issues which impact on her wellbeing
- or by inviting her to dig into systemic issues around ethos and expectations at work, deployment and resources, staffing and support structures.

Interpretative supervision widens the lens of understanding and of exploration and asks 'How can we understand this more fully?'.

The expertise of the interpretative supervisor lies not in knowing how to diagnose or fix things but in being able to facilitate inquiry, wonder and curiosity. The benefit of the approach is that supervisees can come to understand why things are as they are. The downside is that although supervisees may leave sessions more *informed* their situations may be no further *transformed* by this mode of exploration.

The Identity Lens: Who am I/who are we in this story?
A fourth lens through which to conduct supervision is to explore what the presenting story reveals about the supervisee as a person or about their professional identity. And so the key question becomes 'Who are you in this situation?[32] Identity-focused supervision is founded on the principle that supervisees don't so much bring cases to supervision (as often happens in counselling or clinical supervision) but *are themselves the case* that is brought.[33] David Whyte captures supervision through an identity lens beautifully when he states: 'Work is the place where the self meets the world.'[34] And so, if we wanted to help Fiona explore the material she brought to supervision through an identity lens we might ask her:

- who are you in this situation?
- what does the story reveal about you as a person and/or as a practitioner?'
- where did the real Fiona go when you were faking it for others?
- who would you be if you stopped trying so hard?
- who would you be if you got your life back?

The benefits of identity-focused supervision lie in helping supervisees integrate their personal and professional identities such that they can heal splits and dissonances between what happens internally and how they behave in the external world. Nevertheless, the downside is that identity-focused supervision can get lost in introspection and end up over attending to issues of motivation and interiority to the neglect of those 'absent others' who are on the receiving end of the supervisee's practice and for whom the supervisor has a duty of care. Striking a balance is therefore crucial for those who occupy this default approach in supervision.

The Imaginative Lens
A fifth approach to supervision is as much a supervisory modality as it is a supervisory lens. The American poet Emily Dickinson writes:

'Tell all the truth but tell it slant,
Success in Circuit lies'

'Not knowing when the dawn will come, I open every door'[35]

For many supervisees, especially those who can drown in their own words, being invited to explore work issues through methods which 'tell it slant', methods which arise 'out of the box', often brings surprising results. And so, if the solution lens asks supervisees to find a way round things, and the interpretative lens asks the supervisor to step back and understand things in their complexity, supervision through the imaginative lens invites us to

- suspend working things out in our heads
- let go of control
- and allow the unconscious to yield its wisdom.[36]

If we wanted to help Fiona explore the material she brought earlier by 'telling it slant' we could

- invite her to re-tell (or to be more precise), re-*present* her story without words by creating a visual installation using objects or images and then ask her where her eye lands and begin our exploration from there
- or we could ask her to choose something to represent the joy she once had in her work and to place that representation somewhere in the room and then position herself in relation to that
- or we could invite her to use chairs or cushions to explore different parts of herself with one chair being the part of herself that was once fulfilled at work and the other being her current experience and then get each of those parts of the self to speak to and hear from the other.

The benefits of imagination focused – telling it slant - supervision is that it can get to the heart of things very fast and release people when they feel stuck or when staying in their heads doesn't seem to be working. But the downside can be that supervisees get in touch and inadvertently reveal far more about themselves than they might have done through words which some may find disconcerting.

Each of the five lenses I have outlined understands the role and expertise of the supervisor in different ways but none of them are watertight.

Summary of Supervisory Lenses

Lens	Asks supervisor to	Domains of Expertise
Diagnostic	Diagnose	Knowledge & Interpretation
Solution	Fix	Knowledge, Interpretation & Skills
Interpretative	Piece together	Analysis & Interpretation
Identity	Treat practitioner as 'the case'	Exploration & enquiry
Imagination	Explore things 'slant'	Creative exploration & facilitation

- The *Diagnostic* lens asks the supervisor to diagnose for which she needs knowledge and interpretation.

- The *Solution* lens asks her to fix things for which she requires expertise in knowledge, interpretation and skills.

- The *Interpretative* lens asks her to piece things together and in so doing locates her expertise in the fields of contextual analysis and interpretation.

- The *Identity* lens asks her to treat the supervisee 'as the case' that is brought to supervision[37] and requires skills in sensitively exploring and inquiring without trespassing on therapeutic territory.

- And the *Imagination* lens asks her to explore things 'slant' and to be able to facilitate and foster curiosity in creative ways.

What matters, if supervision is to be most effective and truly 'pastoral' not just in name, but in reality, is that supervisors *supervise* not in their own preferred modes but in ways which make the *supervisee* and not the supervisor centre stage. And that requires supervisors to have as rich a repertoire as possible to meet the needs of supervisees some of whom come seeking diagnosis, some solutions, some to piece things together, some to understand themselves better and others 'out of the box' creative exploration.

For Reflection

1. Reflecting on your practice as a supervisor, what is your default lens?

2. What lens is under-developed in your practice?

3. To be more effective in meeting the needs of your supervisees, which lenses would you like to further develop?

Processes

Chapter Five
Pre-transference:
It starts before we meet!

One of the lessons that supervising has taught me is that what happens before we even meet has a massive bearing on what happens in the supervisory room and in our pastoral and supervisory relationships: the stray thought as you read an email from a new supervisee; the things you pick up in that two minute phone call to agree a date and time to meet; the unbidden fantasy you have as you go to answer the doorbell.

What I am naming is pre-transference, that mixter-maxter[38] of random thoughts, feelings, intuitions, fantasies and somatic experiences that arise (apparently from nowhere) and which make the emerging relationship anything but neutral before you have even begun.

At root, transference is quite simply a form of communication by impact. Something from one place or from one relationship gets carried over (transferred) from one place or relationship to another. And how do we know? Because we experience, sense or intuit its impact. And that is exactly what happens with pre-transference. Before we have even met in person, before a session begins, or perhaps just by seeing someone's name in our diaries, an unbidden reaction, thought, feeling or bodily sensation occurs which is highly informative, opaque in meaning and anything but neutral.

- 'Oh great I've got John at 11.'

- 'Oh dash! I've got that group at 2.'
- 'Gosh I hope Jill won't be as boring as last time.'
- 'Better have a good breakfast, I've got the group from hell at 3.'

To the transactional supervisor, the supervisor who dispenses wisdom or knowledge to grateful disciples, pre-transference phenomena are to be ignored as unwelcome and irrelevant interference. But to the relational supervisor, the person who knows that the relationship is the locus of all growth and learning, pre-transference offers a rich stream of unconscious material which is communicated by impact from the supervisee to the supervisor.

But this is far from unproblematic. One of the downsides of working with good, loving people in the caring professions is that they very often ignore or refuse to pay attention to pre-transference experiences out of a mistaken sense that to do so would be to predetermine the agenda and diminish the neutrality with which they should approach the relationship. I take a very different view which sees pre-transference experiences quite simply as information which can be summed up as follows:

When all of me
turns up for you
then I can afford to trust that whatever happens between us
no matter how random,
no matter how off the wall
may be of use to you.
Whereas when my fragmented self,
turns up largely for me,

then whatever goes on within me
is likely to trip us both up.[39]

Objectivity/Subjectivity

Core to what I am talking about is the whole issue of whether supervisors should be objective or subjective. Objectivity in care and supervision has traditionally been valued.

- 'Mind the gap between your story and your client's story'
- 'Be clear whose space you are in'
- 'Get your own needs met outside the care relationship'
- 'Maintain sufficient distance to ensure you don't become embroiled in the other person's process'
- 'Establish good boundaries etc.'

And if that is what we mean by objectivity in supervision then I have no argument whatsoever. The problem however arises when people mistake objectivity for neutrality, for agenda free care and for the only professional way to be in the world. And that to me is simply not the case. As a hospital chaplain I am not neutral about my patients. I want them to get better. And if they can't get better, I want them to cope as best they can with debilitating illness. And if they enter the palliative phase of life, I hope they will die without pain, reconciled with their families and at peace with the world. As a psychotherapist I am not neutral about my clients. I want them to achieve their goals whatever they may be. If that's the freedom to leave an abusive partner, then I lend my hope to that. If the goal is to find meaning out of loss, then I lend my efforts to that. And if – as I have discovered to my cost - the goal is to prove that therapy doesn't work, that no carer can ever be trusted, that positivity is a tyranny, then, even then, I lend myself to that exploration. My care is anything but objective and certainly not neutral. And this is where naïve understandings of Freud and the talk of the counsellor or supervisor as a blank canvas have not served us well. The world of care is agenda-*rich* not agenda-free. Depending on your frame of reference that agenda is called wellbeing or wholeness or human flourishing or salvation or redemption.

Human flourishing
Person centred care does not see people as neutral entities in isolation but as people who are loved, not disposable. It sees humans as joined at the hip, deeply connected, long before they are badged as supervisor and supervisee, carer and cared for. And while there is no place in therapeutic or pastoral care for imposing my will and choices upon another person's life, I have more hesitations about supervisees who claim to be neutral about their clients than about supervisees who (while fostering their client's autonomy) show commitment to their wellbeing. I have come to the conviction that what supervisees need are practitioners who are no longer trying to be objective but who have befriended their subjectivity sufficiently that it has become their primary therapeutic or caring tool.

To return to what I said earlier:

When all of me
mindfully present, recollected and ready

turns up for you
by creating a hospitable space within me for you

then I can afford to trust whatever happens between us
no matter how random,
no matter how off the wall,

may be of use to you.[40]

In other words, when I make you (the supervisee) centre stage, and clear my mind and heart to deeply attend to you (rather than to get my own needs met), then I can allow myself to feel, think and sense things of all kinds which I can *tentatively* offer back to you through appropriately pitched wonderings' according to

- the way *you* learn or process things (ie verbal, metaphorical; pictorial; embodied; analytic) rather than my preferred mode of supervising or teaching;
- your developmental stage, practitioner experience and need;
- the quality of trust that exists in our relationship.

Whereas

When I (supervisor) am not present to myself
through distraction or mindlessness

and don't make space for you (supervisee)
by filling the space with my own insecurities fears, or need for
validation

> then my subjectivity
> *whatever happens within my head, heart, soul or body*
> *as you speak and explore within the session*
>
> is likely to trip me up and hinder you
> *because I have no way of knowing if*
> *that strange thought,*
> *that knot in my stomach,*
> *that fleeting image that popped into my head*
> *arises from you or from me.*[41]

Let me illustrate this with a story from my own supervisory practice.

Some years ago, in the fallow time between Christmas and New year, I received an email from a well-known and eminent practitioner asking if he could come to me for supervision. As I read his email my pre-transference feelings and thoughts were set in train:

> *'What is someone as eminent as him doing asking to see me? I will have nothing to offer him. He is going to find out I am a charlatan and then walk away leaving me exposed as a sham, a fake with nothing to offer. And then what will I do?'*

Of course, I didn't say any of that in my reply to his email but simply offered to meet with him the following Friday at 10 am.

On the appointed day, I woke up nervous and anxious. I hoovered the room where I see people (even though it didn't need it since I had done it the night before); I polished the glass table; set a tray with coffee cups that match rather than my usual random ones. But even after all my preparatory efforts I still could not settle. By 5 minutes to 10 I was agitated, breathing heavily and really struggling to contain myself. At 10 am on the dot he rang my door bell. And as I stretched out my hand to welcome him over the threshold, an elastoplast from his hand became dislodged and ended up on one of my fingers. We were both acutely embarrassed. This was not the way things were meant to begin. He was not even over the threshold. The door was not even shut and already, in that gesture of welcome, a leaking wound had been uncovered, a route to cross infection had been opened and I had blood on my hands.

And in that instant, all my fears about being a charlatan went right out the window and all I knew was that this new relationship – barely a minute old by this point – was not going to start from fear but from deeply human, embarrassing and potentially shaming, bloody contact. The story that unfolded was of a practitioner who felt like a sham and a fake; a charlatan who felt naked, exposed and with nothing to offer.

Suddenly the pre-transference made sense: my reactions to his email; my increasing anxiety as the appointment drew closer; the things I had been experiencing about being a charlatan, about having nothing to offer; of being a sham and a fake were actually my supervisee's thoughts and feelings which had been communicated to me *by impact* as information which would enable me to enter *his* internal world so as to be better able to accompany him as he sought to bear the unbearable in his professional practice.

Pre-transference is an ally. It bears wisdom which we should attend to. Supervisors who are willing to befriend their subjectivity rather than shun it out of a mistaken belief that objectivity and neutrality are to be fostered, can expect to feel, sense and intuit things of all kinds. Learning to trust pre-transferential experiences as informative is itself a form of hospitality which places the other rather than the self at the centre of the encounter. Pre-transference experiences invite us to 'show up'[42] for the other and become more not less present in the room.

For Reflection

1. What pre-transference or threshold experiences have you had as a supervisor?

2. What stray thoughts, feelings or images have arisen before you even met for a first supervision session (email; phone?)

3. What do you notice as you see supervisee's names in your diary or call them to mind?

4. How have such experiences played out in the supervisory relationship?

Chapter Six
Attending to Dynamics

A great deal has been written about dynamics in the helping relationship, much of it from a therapeutic standpoint. As pastoral supervision breaks free from its dependence on the psychological therapies and claims its voice as a distinctive way of supervising across the professions, so too the need arises to articulate key dimensions of the supervisory relationship in ways which do not presume that supervisors have therapeutic training. Indeed, one of the joys of working across the professions, is that pastoral supervision has access to a much wider menu of literature, philosophy and practice than hitherto. And so, when it comes to looking at dynamics within the supervisory relationship one of the things I have found most useful and accessible for people with no therapeutic hinterland is offered by Patrick Lencioni's research from the business world.[43]

What Lencioni found working with professional teams across the globe was considerable disparity between how people at the top and people at the bottom entered into any new work-based project. At its simplest company Directors and middle managers went into any new project looking for a result. So for example if you are IBM then your intended result might be to win over Apple or Microsoft customers. If you are the General Manager of a conference venue, your intended result might be to impress conference delegates such that they could be enticed back in the future. Or if you are the Clinical Director of a healthcare facility, your intended result might be to ensure a culture of safe, effective, person-centred care that will reduce complaints and improve staff morale. But while such results are incontrovertible in and of themselves, what Lencioni found in results-focused organisations was that they often failed to grasp that the workforce at ground level typically viewed new ventures through the lens of personal safety and survival which he places at the base of his triangle and calls 'Trust'.

Trust
And so non-managerial staff at Microsoft might ask 'what's in it for us in pursuing this goal of getting one over Apple?' Staff at the conference venue might wonder what going the extra mile for delegates will mean for them when they are understaffed and underpaid? And practitioners in the healthcare facility, might raise an eyebrow or two at the irony of a dictat from on high about being more person-centred if they don't feel treated as persons by their bosses.

The parallel with supervision is striking. When it comes to new supervisory relationships, whether individual or in groups, supervisors may well begin with clear results in mind: growth in supervisee's personal awareness; increased joy and satisfaction at work; enhanced ability to bring soul, role and context into intentional dialogue; heightened capacity for reflection-in-action etc. New supervisees, on the other hand, might approach the first meeting wondering how they are going to manage being known *and* being safe; how they can allow their practice to be seen while protecting themselves from dissolving inside; and, how they are going 'to bear the intimacy of scrutiny and flourish within it.'[44] Supervision certainly demands trust, but that trust needs to be earned.

Supervisors who take pre-transference seriously need to begin by presuming that trust does *not* exist, and then, actively working from ground zero, foster it at every level. Trust is incremental. It starts in small things. Being clear about times and dates; about venue and access; about fees and reporting systems. Building trust, rather than presuming it, creates connection and increases any chance of engagement and participation.[45] And trust is dismantled when supervisees arrive to find that no attention has been paid to making the environment conducive to learning or to the very basics of hospitality. Trust is the bedrock of supervision but it takes time and effort to build it. It takes even longer when survival [or getting a good report at the end of it] is at stake. If pastoral supervision is to be super *and* visionary, something which expands horizons and transforms practice, then fear is its biggest enemy and trust its greatest ally.

Conflict
What Lencioni's research found was the fear of difference was so great in groups that most try to avoid it all costs

out of a fear that equates difference with conflict. As a consequence many people settle for artificial harmony over constructive debate which leads to a dilution of learning and lowering of expectations. The educationalist Parker J. Palmer writes:

'Differences in an established group are not likely to be particularly threatening but in a group of semi-strangers, differences [can] threaten the group's already flimsy interpersonal structure ... and lead group members to make quick ad-hoc compromises.'[46]

As trust begins to grow, (through a natural process of testing the waters and finding that we didn't drown), differences begin to emerge in the supervisory relationship:

- differences in gender; age; physical ability; orientation; colour;
- differences in educational background;
- differences that are conveyed by the use of street language or formal English;
- differences in learning styles;
- different levels of confidence and self esteem
- different responses to authority figures from previous learning and supportive experiences
- differences in openness to change and ability to act on insight.

One of the most important differences in supervision is the whole area of power within the relationship. Is the supervisor a sage on the stage or a guide by my side? Are supervisees trainees or experts on their own practice?

In the interests of live and let live, many of us 'have been taught to ignore or smooth out differences rather than see them as forces for change'.[47] The antidote to difference, according to Audre Lord is that 'divide and conquer must become define and empower.'[48]

Lencioni's helpful insight is that for relationships to be functional and to have any chance of achieving their stated purposes then leaders (in our case supervisors) need to help participants *step up* the ladder (from trust to facing differences) while being willing themselves to *step down* a rung to attend to the preceding layer. Stepping down a rung on Lencioni's triangle from Results we find the layer of Accountability.

Accountability
Professional life is shot through with accountability. And rightly so. Supervisees are accountable for the delivery of quality care in their work settings; for professional growth and development; for skill enhancement and care plans; and for collaborating with others in the work setting. Likewise, supervisors are accountable for ensuring congruence between their practice and the standards and competencies prescribed by their regulatory bodies, for keeping up to date with developments in the field of supervision and ultimately for ensuring the wellbeing of those with whom the supervisee works. And this is where the middle rung of Lencioni's pyramid is pivotal

Commitment
What Lencioni calls 'committing to decisions' can be understood as establishing 'the *WE* factor' by which I mean, establishing whatever it is that both supervisee *and*

supervisor can wholeheartedly say yes to. I equate what he is saying to that moment in a supervisory relationship when the parties involved move from a series of individual 'I's' to being able to agree on something. Take healthcare for example. Whenever I ask nurses or doctors what they would want for their mums or their children if they were admitted to hospital, what I inevitably hear is something along the lines of 'gold standard care'. That's a *WE* statement expressing a powerfully held and emotionally charged commitment. Similarly, if I ask a care home manager what she wants for her staff, I inevitably hear something along the lines of 'I want them to be well and flourish so that their care for our elderly residents enables them to be well and flourish too.'

These kinds of shared commitments – these yes or *we* statements - enable supervisors to respectfully inquire: 'and what gets in the way of that happening that would make working at our differences (one rung down) worthwhile and upping our accountability (one rung up) possible?' And that is why the middle stage, the stage of shared commitments, is absolutely pivotal to effective supervision.

Lencioni's wisdom (adapted for pastoral supervision) can be summarised as follows:

- When trust is absent supervisors and supervisees become unwilling to be *vulnerable* to each other.

- When people fear that differences will inevitably escalate into conflict then *artificial harmony* replaces robust enquiry and exploration.

- When commitment and shared purpose is lacking, *ambiguity and ambivalence* characterise the supervisory relationship.

- When accountability is avoided, supervisors and supervisees collude with counterproductive behaviours and in so doing lower *expectations and standards*.

- And when insufficient attention is paid to achieving the stated result (of reflecting on the past, in the present for the sake of the future), then personal success, *status and ego* of either party in the supervisory relationship is valued more highly than the supervisee's growth and learning and the wellbeing of those with or for whom the supervisee works.

The converse is also true. When supervisors begin their work with new supervisees - whether in individual or group supervision – presuming the absence of trust while working at doing everything they can to make themselves and the experience trustworthy, then supervisees may feel sufficiently secure to move beyond the very real needs of survival towards establishing a relationship in which shared commitments – to the supervisee's wellbeing and that of those they serve – can be attended to in ways in which differences (one rung down) are attended to and accountability (one rung up) in achieving best practice or the anticipated result can be encouraged.

For Reflection

1. Thinking of those you supervise, which rung on Lencioni's pyramid do you most attend to? Which do you most neglect?

2. What steps do you take to make it possible for the supervisee to trust you? What might you overlook or neglect?

3. How do you actively name rather than gloss over issues of difference?

4. How do you elicit shared commitments in the supervisory relationship?

5. In what ways are you accountable personally and professionally for the integrity of supervision as a practice and a profession?

6. How do you track and monitor your work with supervisees such that they progress towards their personal and professional goals?

Chapter Seven
Structuring the Time

In chapter five I stressed the importance of attending to pre-transference phenomena as valuable sources of information. In chapter six I traced some of the dynamics that typically play out in supervision and underlined the pivotal role of finding shared commitments – the *we* factor – to make the risk taking worthwhile. In this chapter I offer a way of structuring the supervisory session itself from arrival to departure.

In presenting this blended model I make no claim to originality. I draw on many sources and especially the cyclical model offered by Steve Page and Val Wosket[49] to which I add attention to hospitality, presence and wisdom all of which are essential if supervision is to be soulful.

Mapping a Supervision Session
As an intentional space, supervision has a clear structure characterised by six processes outlined overleaf

Hosting and Containing focuses on the kind of hospitality which enables transformative learning. This includes attention to the ethical framework, organization culture, immediate environment and quality of interpersonal relationship between participants.

Eliciting and Focusing is not only about getting the work into the room but about identifying the energy or impulse that will make reflection worthwhile, i.e. What is it in particular about this that makes it worth looking at here today?

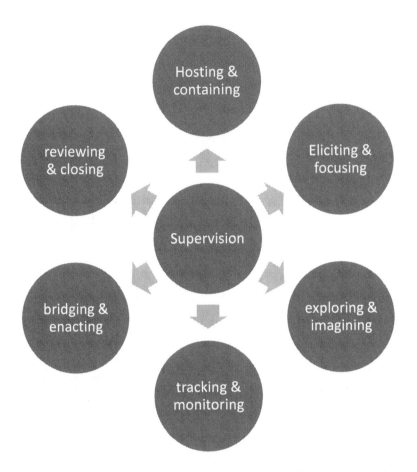

Exploring and Imagining. Once a focus has been established, exploring and imagining becomes a playful and creatively fertile place in which to try out ideas and ways of working. It is also the place in which stray thoughts, fantasies, images and metaphors can be aired.

Tracking and Monitoring. Tracking is both a discreet moment in the reflective cycle and something that runs through the whole session. It is a way of monitoring that what is happening is matching what it is needed within the allotted time.

Bridging and Enacting are reminders that we reflect on work from the *past*, in the *present* in order to change and enhance work in the *future*. A bridge is built out from the reflective time and back into the world of everyday practice. Enacting names the first steps to be taken.

Reviewing and Closing is the process of naming what has been learned through reflection and the drawing of a line on the exploration. In supervision, closing well is just as important as beginning well.

Each of the six components can be unfolded as follows.

Hosting and Containing – supervision as hospitality

Hosting and containing can be summed up as attentive hospitality. If guests are coming for dinner it would be inhospitable to have no food in the house to give them when they arrive. Similarly, if guests are vegetarian it would be inhospitable to serve them steak. Hospitality requires anticipating what guests may need and being ready to accommodate those needs. Likewise, hospitable supervision gives central place to the supervisee and requires the supervisor to be eccentric ie to stand back (*ex*) from the centre (*centrum*) to make space for the other.

According to Parker J. Palmer, learning spaces have three essential dimensions: openness, boundaries and an air of hospitality. Openness requires clearing away the clutter of being occupied with the past and worrying about the future to make space for the present, the 'now' of this moment. As Palmer reminds us, however, 'the openness of a space is created by the firmness of its *boundaries*'. Since supervision offers an intentional structure for learning and not what Palmer calls 'an invitation to confusion and chaos' clarity of purpose, role, use of time and expectation all need to be spelt out. Furthermore, since supervision involves an intricate conversation between practice, practitioner and working context, this kind of learning can be challenging and unsettling. To enable supervision to remain a learning place, it requires to be conducted in an air of hospitality which involves 'receiving each other, our struggles, our new-born ideas, with openness and care'. Hospitable supervision 'will be a place where every stranger and every strange utterance is met with welcome'. [50] For the hospitable supervisor, hosting and containing invites attention to six components:

A physical environment conducive to reflection.
The physical environment is often neglected in the literature on supervision. This may be a reflection of the therapeutic stable from which much of it arises in which it is assumed that supervision is conducted by mature and experienced counsellors and therapists who do not need such a reminder. However, since much pastoral supervision takes place outwith clearly defined therapeutic frames of reference, it is worth considering basic questions such as – If I was coming to this space to talk about something that really mattered to me would this room help or hinder me exploring it? Are these the kind of chairs that encourage the exploration of work or a cosy chat? Is the room warm enough for a comfortable hour together? Will we be disturbed? Have intrusions been anticipated (phones switched off, 'room in use' indicated etc.)

Physical, cognitive, psychological and spiritual presence.
Relational presence is of the essence in supervision. No matter how ideal the physical environment or the skill of

the supervisor, supervision simply will not be possible if those involved cannot relate to each other. While supervisors cannot be held responsible for the psychological make-up of supervisees, they are ethically responsible for their own part in making room within their own hearts and minds to welcome their guests. Mindful attentiveness on the part of the supervisor prior to arrival will afford supervisees a space between past and future practice to attend to whatever is on their mind. Supervisors are truly present when they have cleared a space within their own busy heads and hearts to 'lend' themselves mentally, affectively and spiritually to the other. Without this inner spaciousness, supervisors will be unable to make intentional use of themselves and will leave their supervisees cheated. They will also model a lack of presence to supervisees – who may repeat that pattern with their clients.

Clarity about the purpose of the time together is often lacking in cross-professional supervision. Since the territory and contours of supervision are still largely unknown in many disciplines, the first task of supervision is to teach people what the space is for. Those who present themselves as supervisees need to discover whether supervision is really what they are looking for, or would personal counselling or life coaching be more suited to their needs. Clarity of purpose frees supervisees to know what to bring to sessions and what to reflect on with others elsewhere. It also frees supervisors to note issues of therapeutic or managerial significance without adopting the role of therapist or manager. As supervisees develop reflexivity, personal or therapeutic issues may emerge. Being clear about what belongs where makes for good supervisory hygiene.

A mutually agreed contract or covenant for the work.
The covenant or contract *for working* needs to be co-constructed. What is the supervisor responsible for? What is the supervisee responsible for? How often are they to meet? How long will meetings last? Are expectations clear about payment and how it is to be made? Is there a cancellation policy? Is there a contract for dealing with issues of fitness to practice or for breaks in practice? Is the work ongoing or finite? Is review built in?

A framework of ethical practice underpinning everything.
The entire relationship and all the processes that serve it need to be held within an explicit ethical framework rather than a vague desire to do good and cause no harm. By what code of practice does the supervisor operate? To whom could a supervisee raise issues of concern about the supervisor? Conversely is the supervisory contract an hermetically sealed private affair between the two parties or are there contractual or organisational factors to consider. Are reports to be written? Are there any legal implications for the work? Is the supervisor covered by professional indemnity insurance etc.

Eliciting and Focusing
Nothing does more to kill the energy in supervision than an anxious supervisor who alights on the first thing a supervisee says in a session and presumes to make that the focus for the session. Sometimes supervisees come knowing exactly what they want to talk about and what they are looking for in wanting to explore it. Sometimes they come knowing that a particular incident or encounter has 'stayed with them' and tugged at their mind or heart but cannot identify why it matters or what it relates to. And sometimes people come not knowing

where to begin. This can be for a variety of reasons. Those who are new to supervision may not have the tools to sift through weeks of practice to know what to bring. Those who are overwhelmed by their work may be aware that a decision to bring one issue to supervision closes the door on a cluster of other issues and may find it difficult to know which to choose. Others again may be sufficiently detached from their work to allow it to impinge upon their mental and spiritual energies all of which points to the following essential components of eliciting and focussing:

What are you bringing?
The first duty of the supervisor is to teach the supervisee how to use the space called supervision within which eliciting a supervisory question or issue is paramount. The question 'what are you bringing to supervision?' can be answered in a number of ways. Oftentimes a supervisee will alight on a particular experience: 'being bored listening to someone's story', 'chairing a meeting and going blank when asked a question', 'not knowing my way round something'. At other times what supervisees bring is not so much a particular issue as an aspect of themselves in the work: 'I used to love nursing but right now the pressure is unbearable', 'I feel at a professional crossroads', 'I have had a busy month since we last met but right now I feel blank'. When supervisees simply do not know what to bring, there are useful tools for getting the work into the room such as six minute journaling exercises; choosing a postcard which resonates with their current professional experience; making an installation using objects, stones or buttons to represent their work; or drawing a time line of professional highs and lows.

Why are you bringing it here?
Wherever supervision takes place the word 'work' is
written above the door. Personal and home issues do
arise in supervision but need to be respectfully and
reverently handled in so far as they impinge on the
supervisee's ability to work effectively. There is a
humility built into supervision which recognises that it is
only one form of supportive relationship with its own
particular focus and set of skills. Supervisors need to
protect the integrity and limitations of their role no matter
how hard supervisees push them to play the therapist or
spiritual guide. Nevertheless, establishing the legitimacy
of an issue is only the first step in supervision. Further
exploration is needed to know why someone chooses to
bring an issue to supervision rather than to a line
manager, work colleague or personal friend.

Why are you bringing it today?
The question may seem pedantic and may not always be
asked in such an explicit way, but supervisors will do well
to listen between the lines for hints of an answer. Is the
issue urgent and requiring immediate solution? ('I am
giving a talk next week about X and feel stuck'.) Is the
issue recurring and therefore presenting itself for
exploration now? ('This was the third time that week I
had told a parent that they had no idea what pressure we
teachers were under.') Is the issue impeding other work
from happening? ('I can't get what has happened to L out
of my mind and feel I am neglecting all the other kids in
the youth club.') Asking why today will help focus the use
of time.

What do you want in bringing it?

A supervisee who can answer this question is well on their way to insight. 'I am looking for a second opinion that what I did was not off the wall' (supervision as validation). 'I feel ashamed about messing up at work and need to unravel the mess (supervision as catharsis). 'I feel chuffed that I managed to confront my fears for a change and speak up for myself (supervision as bearing witness). 'I have been over this again and again in my head and even talked it through with colleagues but I fear I may be deceiving myself (supervision as courageous conversation). People have many reasons for bringing their work to supervision a fraction of which is voiced explicitly. Practitioners' developmental stages have a part to play in what they might be looking for. For example, a novice practitioner may be seeking direct instruction (what do I do, what do I say) whereas a mature practitioner may simply be looking for someone to afford them the quality of hearing that they themselves offer others (consultative support).[51]

Agreeing a focus.

Agreeing a focus is an expression of hospitality. Just as a host would not give a guest who requested a beer a cup of tea, so too a supervisor who has elicited a focus needs to respond to that focus and not follow their own interests. In practice this means that once the supervisory issues or focus has been established every subsequent intervention needs to be attuned to that issue. This requires discipline (the agenda is set by the supervisee and not the supervisor); repertoire (a range of ways of going deeper into the issue that has been identified) and monitoring (are we dealing with the real issue here or getting side tracked).

Exploring and Imagining

While exploration is the very air that therapists and counsellors breathe, it comes less naturally to many others. In practice, many people faced with a problem immediately begin scrambling around for a solution. While this is sometimes exactly what is required, overuse of quick fix solutions renders exploration redundant. When it comes to supervision we are not dealing so much with problems that need to be fixed as people who need to be accompanied. This is based on the wisdom that the first authority on the client is the client. The second is the practitioner and only the third is the supervisor. Admittedly, supervisees do not always present themselves and their dilemmas in that way but effective supervisors do well to remember that and resist the projections to which they are regularly subjected.

Without due attention to exploration, supervision risks becoming an advice shop in which a wise all-knowing person (the supervisor) dispenses wisdom to a less experienced person (the supervisee) who is expected to be grateful. Such outdated models of supervision accentuate the power dynamic between the two parties and invite dependency and obedience rather than professional development and transformative learning. Exploration accounts for about two thirds of the time allotted for supervision, Since there is an abundance of literature on how to explore issues in supervision I shall simply note some of the key points here.

Tell me.

The 'Telling' approach favours speech and cognition. Thus a supervisor may say: 'Describe the scene for me. Who was there? Where were you in the room? Were you standing or sitting? Tell me how you were feeling before the incident occurred. Talk me through your thought processes, the inner commentary which was running in your head as the scene unfolded? Tell me your stray thoughts or fantasies about the person you were dealing with. Tell me what you would say to your client if there were no holds barred. Tell me who she reminds you of. Tell me about other times in your life where you have had to face similar things.' Supervisors need to be attentive to the possibility that the 'tell me' approach can establish a pattern of question and answer or be experienced as forensic investigation and need to use it only in so far as it enables, rather than limits, exploration.

Show me.
'Showing' approaches invite people to get underneath the stories they tell to the heart of the matter. Asking supervisees to 'show' the situation they are trying to explore using images, objects, art, music or movement can free them 'from the tunnel of words to find colour, energy, creativity and a sense of mystery which is so often lacking in the practice of supervision.'[52] A supervisor might say: 'Using any of the objects you have in your bag show me the team you are referring to. Show me that knot in your stomach that you are describing. Show me what losing the thread means. Show me where in your body that feeling resides. Close your eyes and make a sound which expresses that moment you are trying to get me to understand. Choose a card to depict what it was like to be in the chair at that meeting and another to indicate where you would rather have been.' When situations are explored in this way new meaning can emerge in quite surprising ways. This is what John Williams calls the 'boo' factor of expressive supervision.[53] Supervisors working

with telling approaches need to offer gentle but firm containment since the unconscious is often accessed quickly and deeply through this manner of exploration. Remaining true to the role of supervisor may involve some delicate negotiation here. Supervisors will also need to be aware that some of their supervisees will be 'act hungry' and relish the opportunity to show their work in this way but be less keen to draw out the implications for action that result from insights gained.

Exploring the impact.
Every story impacts upon its hearers. Some stories excite us, some bore us. Some intrigue, some capture our imagination, some appal or horrify us. The impact of a story told in supervision provides invaluable information. Social convention allows for certain impacts to be voiced. Stories which generate a 'wow' factor are welcomed while those which leave us feeling 'yuk' are often left hanging in the air. Feeding back to a supervisee the impact that an aspect from their 'then and there' professional story has had on you 'here and now' can be very illuminative. Consider for example a supervisor saying to a supervisee: 'I was totally engrossed by what you were saying until it flashed through my mind that you might be having me on.' One result would be that the supervisee takes the feedback personally and is offended. If that happened it could mean that the earlier stage of hosting and containing and Lencioni's guidance on trust needs to be revisited. This could be because the supervisor has not paid enough attention to building a relationship conducive to learning or that the supervisor has not pitched their feedback in a way that the supervisee cannot receive. (It could of course just be that the supervisee is feeling particularly vulnerable today for

whatever reason.) However if however hosting and containing is secure, and the eliciting and focusing stage has been well handled, then the feedback 'I was totally engrossed by what you were saying until it flashed through my mind that you might be having me on' might stop the supervisee in their tracks and lead them to at least ponder whether the supervisor's experience of being engrossed and duped in rapid succession resonates with their own experience of working with the client or scenario they have presented in supervision. In short 'exploring the impact' is my laicisation of what the therapeutic world handles under the specialised language of transference, countertransference and parallel process.

Image and Metaphor.
Sometimes the impact of what is presented manifests within those who listen as stray thoughts (must check my bank account to see if she has paid), distractions (wonder what is on TV tonight), images (she looks haunted today) or metaphors (this is Humpty Dumpty all over again). A supervisor who failed to clear their head and heart to make room for the supervisee before she arrived will be disabled by such occurrences and unable to discern whether they arise in out of the supervisee's material or from their own lack of presence. Conversely a supervisor who is ready to greet her guest will know that this strange and apparently random information belongs not to her but to the supervisee and can therefore tentatively offer it for exploration.

Somatic resonance.
Strictly speaking, somatic resonance is a particular form of communication by impact but I have singled it out in order to accentuate the importance of the supervisor

being fully present – including bodily and energetically – to those with whom they work. Thus, for example a supervisor may suddenly be overwhelmed by tiredness, a tiredness which has no basis in fact since they have slept well and were felling rested until the supervisee began to speak about their work with a particular client. Feeding back that tiredness as information (without interpretation) is likely to interrupt the narrative and in so doing raise the possibility that something tiring, or energy sapping is going on in the situation being explored or more generally since tiredness is non-verbal, that something is not being said and is not getting through by use of words in the session. When, for example as supervisor, I get a stitch in my side, a sudden stiffness in my neck, sweaty palms, my first task is to ask whether this somatic experience belongs to me or the person I am accompanying. If it belongs to me then I can note it and park it in order to give X my full attention but if I am clear that it does not belong to me then I need to ponder its significance. Does the stiffness in my neck intensify or diminish the longer we speak? Does the stitch in my side come and go or remain constant? At some point in the session the time comes for me as supervisor to share what is going on with the supervisee. 'I have had a stitch in my side for the last five minutes. I wonder if that has anything to do with what you are describing.' 'My hands have become increasingly sweaty as I listen to you talking about that meeting. Does that connect in anyway with the experience you are describing?' While somatic resonance should not be *sought* in supervision nor should it be *resisted* when it emerges unbidden. Not all supervisors are susceptible to this form of communication by impact but those who are would do well to monitor this in supervision on supervision.

Tracking and Monitoring
Tracking is both a discreet moment in the reflective cycle and a way of monitoring and paying attention to what is happening in the supervisory space as a whole. Tracking has two components:

1. charting the progress of the supervisory issue
2. monitoring that what happens within the allotted time by way of exploring and imagining meets the needs of the presenter and does not dissolve into a general discussion of a topic which belongs in a seminar room.

Within tracking and monitoring five characteristics can be identified:

Interest.
Something caused the supervisee to choose this rather than some other issue to bring today. If the eliciting and focusing stage has been well handled then it will have become clear why this particular issue is of interest to the supervisee. Monitoring what happens to that interest as the session progresses will help maintain momentum. Similarly, supervisors should track their own interest level noting when they become more interested and when less so. If supervision is conducted in a group it is sometimes worth explicitly asking group members what catches their interest in what someone is presenting and then asking the presenter if any of that feedback resonates with them.

Energy.

Tracking energy is closely related to monitoring interest. A loss of energy in supervision may indicate a number of things: that the issue lacked sufficient 'charge' to merit sustained reflection (in which case the option of revising the supervisory question always exists); that loss of energy is a factor in the issue that is currently being presented (a form of parallel process); that the situation carries within it an investment in remaining stuck (for example a client who does not want to get better). As with all interventions, tracking and monitoring energy is best used as a form of noticing or wondering (rather than as a categorical statement) which gives the presenter room to manoeuvre.

(Re)Focusing.

A focusing intervention could be along the lines of: 'You said you wanted to explore why you find it so hard to visit the care home. With the group's help you clarified that it was not the care home itself that you found difficult but having to deal with Molly the manager. When I invited you to show us how you felt when Molly was on duty you chose the handcuffs and when I invited you to show us how you felt when she wasn't on duty you chose the windmill. I noticed the difference in your body energy when you were holding the windmill and when you were holding the handcuffs. For the last five minutes you have been talking about the youth club you visit and I am wondering if these things are related or if we have gone off track?'

Engagement.

Supervision is an activity for consenting adults in private. As such it requires engagement. One of the paradoxes of the promotion of supervision across the professions is that some people now come to supervision without any investment in the relationship that is required or without any commitment to seeking insight or improving their practice. As a consequence, supervisors can find themselves *over*compensating and tiring themselves out by doing too much of the work in the session. Ambivalent engagement can also arise when something the supervisor or group members say or do inadvertently presses a supervisee's buttons and causes them to retreat in self-defence. When it becomes clear that this has happened and that the supervisee is not willing to explore that defence within the supervision session the supervisor has little hope of going any further. In a group setting the supervisor might choose to close that particular supervisee's work at this point and take the remaining time to work with the resonances group members have found in the story originally presented. This will take the spotlight off the presenter allowing them time to regroup and (possibly) re-engage.

Timing.

Tracking time relates to safe containment. Simple interventions are helpful here: 'We have an hour together today I wonder what the best use of that time is for you?'; 'We are half way through our time together so I just want to check that we are doing what you need us to do with you today'; 'We have ten minutes left so I want to ask if you are any closer to finding a way forward?'; 'I am afraid we are now out of time and there are still unanswered questions but we do have to stop there.' Another aspect of tracking time is to monitor who is taking the air space and who might not have been able to speak: 'We are half way through our time and I notice that we have only heard from three people in the group. Would anyone else like to come in at this point?' or in individual supervision: 'I notice you have spoken continuously for the last thirty minutes and just wonder if you want anything from me today.'

Bridging & Enacting

Bridging and Enacting are reminders that we reflect on work from the *past*, in the *present* in order to change and enhance work in the *future*. At this stage in the session we seek to build a bridge from reflection-on-action to the world of everyday practice the supervisee will enter when they leave the session. Enacting is about supervisees articulating first steps expressive of the insight they have found in the session. The literature of coaching offers a great deal of practical insight and wisdom in this area.

Building a Bridge.

Bridges span two places. Supervisory bridges span the place of exploration and discovery (the supervision session) and the place of enactment (work place). Bridges can be permanent or temporary, made of stone, steel, wood or rope. So too supervisory bridges may be emergency solutions or elaborate constructions which will take many years to accomplish. However construed, bridges build professional confidence in helping supervisees recover a sense of empowerment in taking something back from the exploratory session to the work place.

Building what is needed.
Some bridges are built within the supervisee herself. 'I
know I can't do anything to change the situation but
knowing that you will be standing there cheering me on
from the side lines already makes a big difference. That is
the bridge I am going to hold on to'. Other bridges are
conceptual 'I am going from here today laying down the
handcuffs and holding that windmill in my hand. I am
going to put a windmill as my screensaver on my
computer to remind me what I found here today.'

Support for building.
Coming as it does at the end of a session this question is
deliberately framed positively 'what will support you'
without the expected rejoinder 'and what will impede
you?' This is partly to do with the supervisory process
(the time of exploration has come to an end we are now in
a time of decisive action) and the economy of time (to look
at the question from both sides would take longer and
impact on the earlier stages in the session.) Much more
importantly however, the positive tone of the question is
expressive of a philosophical stance which focuses on
assets rather than deficits and sees supervisees as highly
resourced people capable of making informed choices for
themselves. Using the tools of appreciative enquiry,
asking what makes for well-being enables the session to
end on an empowering note.

First steps.
The question of first steps in building a bridge from
reflection to practice is often self-evident in which case it
does not have to be asked. However, if the bridge that has
been articulated is overly ambitious asking about first
steps may induce a sense of reality into the equation and

therefore save the supervisee from a sense of failure or inadequacy. 'In a few minutes this session will end and you will leave here to go back to work. What baby step could you take as you begin to enact that much bigger desire you have?'

Next steps.
Again this is often self-evident. Simple interventions may help. 'You have realised today that you feel inadequate as a counsellor because you haven't kept up with your professional development and have said that even admitting that to me today is a huge first step. So what would you're your next step to be?' … 'And by when will you have done that?

Reviewing and Closing
Reviewing is the process of naming what has been learned through reflection and closing, the drawing of a line on the exploration. In supervision, closing well is just as important as beginning well.

Reviewing works at different levels. In the here and now of the session that is coming to an end, it traces the journey in which both parties have shared from the supervisee's arrival through to her imminent departure. It notes cairns and signposts along the way: that moment of stuckness; the belly laugh that took everyone by surprise; the stray thought which moved things on; the silence that was shared for a few minutes; the moment of connection etc. Reviewing also works at another level in fostering the supervisee's internal supervisor and reflexivity and in implicitly offering them another tool to use when appropriate with their own clients.

Insight gained by Supervisee.
Being able to name the learning that has taken place is a key moment in supervision understood as transformational learning. Sometimes insight is crystal clear: 'I am no longer a four year old in the playground. Bullies should be resisted.' At other times insight may be embryonic and inarticulate: 'I can't quite put my finger on it but I know its something to do with recognising the difference between caring for my colleagues and being a complete sponge which soaks everything up'. Leaving supervision able to name insight provides a reparative experience for people whose professional lives are often entangled with stories of diminishment of one kind or another.

Insight gained by the supervisor/group.
There is an alchemy in pastoral supervision which often results in mutual reciprocity: when one person takes the risk of bringing their work to the loving and critically supportive eye of another, both parties benefit from the encounter. In group supervision this is sometimes articulated as follows: 'when one person is supervised every member of the group receives supervision'. Underlying this is the truth that when supervision is conducted within an 'air of hospitality' the truth-telling risk of the presenter evokes (albeit at times in an unconscious manner) reflection within their hearers. In group supervision it is good to leave time at the end of the session to invite those present to name any insights gained for their own practice as result of accompanying the presenter in an exploration of his or her issue. Supervisors need to contain this well lest it turn into grandstanding or competing stories. *Insight* is what is invited not story telling. In individual supervision it can

also sometimes be valuable for supervisees to hear what supervisors have learned or been reminded of through the work explored. And even when it is not appropriate to voice this with supervisees, an hospitable supervisor can note to themselves what gift their guest brought them today.[54]

Practicalities.
Being clear about the date of the next meeting and any expectations involved helps supervisees know that their work lies within an ongoing intentional rather than opportunistic relationship. Dealing with practicalities within the time together always protects leakage into phone calls and emails between sessions and models the kind of containment supervisees would normally be expected to have with their clients.

Saying Goodbye.
Un-negotiated endings play havoc in people's lives. Many people are drawn to seek help because of unsatisfactory endings: a sudden death, unexpected loss of a job; relationship breakdown; the hanging up of a phone; the slamming of a door. People who have known care as a result of such events often go on to become carers themselves. Supervision offers a chance to model endings that can be healthy, anticipated and negotiated. Managing the micro-endings of each session well will incrementally strengthen the quality of the relationship (for as long as it continues) and play a part in enabling the final goodbye when it comes to an end. As with all aspects of supervision, knowing who you are working with will determine when those goodbyes come. Some supervisees will continue the session right to the front door no matter how many goodbyes you voice. Others know that when

you stand up the session is over and will walk in silence to the door to say goodbye there.

The full cycle of supervision
While hosting and containing, eliciting and focusing, exploring and imagining all happen in sequence, seeing and noticing, wondering and musing, connecting and realizing may happen in any order whatsoever as the session progresses. Similarly tracking and monitoring take place throughout the session in implicit and explicit ways. Time must be safe guarded to facilitate bridging and enacting which is crucial to the process of turning insight into action. Reviewing and closing however brief close the space and help the supervisee return to their daily work once more.

For Reflection

1. In what ways do you attend to hospitality as a supervisor (physical environment, psychological environment, agenda setting etc?)

2. What do you use to elicit a focus? Image cards? Journaling exercises? Silence? Items in the room? Prompt questions?

3. What are your default exploratory modalities? Narration? Small world? Physical embodiment? Internal wise guide?

4. Do you find yourself tracking and paraphrasing your supervisees or do you invite them to track themselves (ie what is the most important thing you have heard yourself say? Or what have you noticed as you have recounted that story?)

5. How do you help supervisees bridge and enact insights found in the session? Images on their phones? Screensaver captions? Internalised memory?

6. How does the end of the session mirror the hospitality which marked the beginning of the session?

Perspectives

Chapter Eight
Vulnerability:
A gift to be unwrapped, not shunned

'You won't get to courage without walking through vulnerability'.[55]

Brené Brown

Conscious that people process and reflect in different ways three things come to mind in exploring the theme of vulnerability as a gift in supervision: an image, a poem and a film clip.

The image comes from a range of greetings cards which feature two older ladies called Irene and Gladys who go around art galleries commenting on the paintings. My favourite card depicts them standing, arm in arm, in their ubiquitous purple and lime green woolly hats before a rather voluptuous naked woman with Irene saying to Gladys: 'That reminds me, you going to Pilates on Tuesday?' Now that, to me, is an image of vulnerability that hasn't been shunned because the people who accept and embrace their vulnerability are the ones who can laugh at themselves.

The poem is Janet Morley's 'The bodies of grown ups' which includes these wonderful lines:

The bodies of grownups
come with stretchmarks and scars
faces that have been lived in ...
... flesh that is particular
and obviously mortal ...

and yet ...
my heart aches
for that grace of longing
that flows through bodies
no longer straining to be innocent
but yearning for redemption.[56]

The film clip is from *The Greatest Showman* which tells the story of PT Barnum who wants to create a circus and recruits the weird and wonderful sights that used to feature in the old fashioned circus: the bearded lady; the dwarf; the giant; the Siamese twins etc.

As the story begins, it is clear that Barnum is in it for fame and for fortune. But to his and everyone's surprise, what happens is that the people he gathers to be his performers find a sense of acceptance and belonging within the circus troupe, a sense of family and of being at home in being together.

The film was released on 28 December 2017. I doubt for a minute that the film producers intended it or even knew about it, but in the western Christian calendar 28 December is Holy Innocents day, the day which commemorates how King Herod was so threatened by the news that a new-born baby might grow up and overthrow his power, that he arranged a mass murder of all male babies under two years of age.[57] And if that is not a story of vulnerability that has never been owned I wonder what is. Who was more vulnerable, King Herod or the babies?

Going back to the release date, I imagine the film was brought out on 28 December because it fell between Christmas and New Year when a lot of people are off work and free to spend disposable income going to the cinema. But delving a little deeper in unwrapping rather than shunning our vulnerability, there is nothing like the season of Christmas to reinforce the reality that the deal – especially the let's play happy families deal – is often far from ideal, and there's nothing like family holiday time to remind people just how fragile life, love and relationships actually are.

The film is very powerful at all sorts of levels but especially in today's world where looks are everything and in which if going to the gym won't give you the perfect figure or physique there's at least Botox and cosmetic surgery. And so, in that perfect 'body image is everything' culture, it is really curious that this film has been so successful and has spoken so powerfully to so many people since it flies in the face of the dominant message.

The film has two leading ladies. The first is Jenny Lund, a stunningly attractive woman with a perfect figure. She is an opera singer who sings in the classical style and has a large following of fans. She travels the world enjoying everyone's adulation and is a classic super celebrity. But no matter how may encores she gets, no matter how many standing ovations she receives, no matter how many people queue at the stage door for her autograph, she never quite feels that she is good enough and the appreciation with which she is showered never sinks in. In short, she never embraces her vulnerability and consigns herself to a life of addictive self-wounding.

The other leading lady in the film is a bearded lady who is as broad as she is round. What is striking is that unlike the opera singer we never learn her name. She has lived her life in the shadows, hidden away, unseen, unknown, unnamed. And when we first meet her she is singing, behind closed doors, working in a laundry out of sight. She sings from the heart in a deep, throaty, soulful way that only those who have suffered can. She is not used to being seen in public and is terrified of taking to the stage. She shuns the limelight and is reluctant to come out of the shadows. But gradually as she embraces her vulnerability she becomes the person everyone else in the circus rallies around. She is the leader of the vulnerable, the champion of the underdog. Her message is summed up in the anthem 'This is me' with the lyrics:

> When the sharpest words
> wanna cut me down
> I'm gonna send a flood,
> gonna drown them out
> I am brave, I am bruised
> I am who I'm meant to be, this is me.
> Look out 'cause here I come
> and I'm marching on to the beat I drum.
> I'm not scared to be seen
> I make no apologies, this is me.[58]

The film has taken the English speaking world by storm and that anthem which sold over 5 million copies in the first year, has helped so many people who have hidden themselves away to know that there is a place for them and to dare to imagine coming out from the shadows. The song gives voice to people whose experience is that society doesn't want their broken parts and that no one will love them as they are. That anthem speaks for many carers, supervisors included, who have 'learned to be ashamed of all their scars'.

In the film those scars are visible, physical and engraved in people's bodies but no less shame-making are our own invisible scars, those invisible bruises we carry in our hearts, those dents to our confidence that we are lovable, acceptable. And that line 'I am brave, I am bruised, I am who I'm meant to be' captures beautifully what it is to see vulnerability as a gift to be unwrapped rather than shunned.

I wept my way through that film when I first saw it and continue to be deeply moved by it. Why? Because I recognise my story in it. And I recognise the stories of so many people I have sat with over the years at bedsides, in counselling rooms, in churches, in care facilities and in supervision. Sadly, some of them buckled under the pressure and gave up the ghost, withdrawing like wounded animals into the subterfuge, living lives of hiding or just about scraping through by self-medicating on drink or drugs or sex or gambling. Nor do supervisors come off lightly since experience confirms that those who make caring for others their life's work, often self-medicate by equally damaging addictive behaviours which are all the more deceptive by having the appearance of respectability about them. At least those addicted to drink or drugs can go to 12 step meetings, but where do religious leaders who are serially addicted to the next big sweaty project for God go? Where do workaholic social activists go to admit that their care for others has become compulsive and arises no longer from soulfulness but from a need to be needed, to be validated or well thought of? And where is the 12 step recovery programme for carers who have turned care into an addiction? Where are the support groups for supervisors who need to get sober 'one day at a time'?

Thankfully addiction is not the full story. Hopefully we each know care professionals who have embraced the truth of their lives, accepted their limitations and long since given up trying to be in control, people who find intrinsic worth in themselves and not only in the work they do. Such people stand as beacons to the rest of us of what it means to live soulfully and not by our own productivity. In my experience such people have gained that serenity, not by being born with silver spoons in their mouths but by hard knocks in life. These are the kind of people Katherine McKennitt is talking about when she writes

'Every time I witness a strong person, I want to know: What dark did you conquer in your story? Mountains do not rise without earthquakes.'[59]

Those words bring to mind countless supervisees I have supported over the years. On the face of it they were supposed to be the people in need and I was supposed to be the helper. But the truth is – unbeknown to them – many of them were actually my teachers, my spiritual guides, my mentors: bearers of a message that offered me another way of living, of doing and of being for which I am deeply grateful.

Vulnerability shunned
In the early days of my supervisory practice, supervisees often expressed a sense of guilt about things they had done. They could point back to some action they had taken for which they felt responsible and for which they felt morally culpable. What I have noticed in recent years is that people increasingly walk through my door not so much with guilt as with a sense of deep personal shame.

And whereas guilt can be traced back to something someone has done or said or omitted to do, shame is much more pervasive and much harder to eradicate as it often has no obvious root or fixed point in a person's history but involves a sense of just not being good enough as a person, not quite the real thing, not as good as everyone else, or of living a life that is not as valid as everyone else's. Sadly it is often the most talented and gifted human beings who are susceptible to shame: people who are wholehearted, people who are really committed, people who take their responsibilities seriously.

Shame has been around for a long time and has quite a pedigree. Biblical scholars point out that the very first time God speaks to a human being, as recorded in Genesis 3.9 it is to ask: 'Where are you?' to which Adam replies on behalf of himself and the woman 'we are hiding because we are naked'. God's response is filled with pathos: 'Who told you that you were naked?', 'Who told you that you had to hide?' We might add in our imaginations: 'Who told you that you had to be ashamed? Who told you that you were not good enough the way you are?'

According to the story, Adam and Eve hid their shame with fig leaves and in so doing started a whole fig leaf industry which has been operating 24/7 ever since. Over the centuries, the form fig leaves take has mutated to keep up with social, political and personal fads but the fig leaf industry is alive and thriving. Faced with a sense of inner nakedness or inner shame, it is not surprising that so many people engage in addictive self-wounding which they try to hid behind fig leaves of workaholism; over-eating; overdoing it at the gym; alcohol abuse; chasing the next emotional high; sexual licence without responsibility; hiding behind God and religion. There are all sorts of drugs of choice around with which to drown out the painful stuff inside.

There's a vast literature available in the specialist field of addiction but in simple terms what I have I come to understand is this:

- What we don't befriend becomes a fiend.
- What we don't anoint will disappoint.
- What we don't express gets repressed.
- What we refuse to own will own us.[60]

And so intentionally staying within a pastoral rather than a therapeutic paradigm my lay man's framework for handling patterns of addictive self-wounding comes down to this:

- *Dissociation* – refusing to face what's real
- *Vacation* – taking a break from what's real
- *Integration* – facing up to the fact that the real is not the ideal without turning it into an ordeal

Dissociation
Dissociation is about denying what's real by splitting off from what is really going on, maintaining the unreal by some form of self-medication. For some, the drug of choice is alcohol, food, substances, gambling or sex. But just as dangerous are those supposedly 'acceptable' addictions of workaholism, never taking time off, saying yes to every invitation which are all forms of distraction by distraction by distraction which prevent us from facing the truth about ourselves: the truth that we are

vulnerable; that we hurt; that we are limited, that we are glorious.[61]

Vacation

A second way of handling addictive self-wounding may be termed vacation. Vacation is what happens when we take a break from a symptom but never get to the root cause. Thus I give up smoking but still crave an instant fix; I start binge dieting and lose weight but don't feel any better inside; I do another course of study but still feel incompetent; I chase a promotion but still feel inadequate when I get it.

Taking a vacation from our patterns of self-wounding is like going in and out of a revolving door, leaving one thing that's bad for us inside and coming out with another one instead; taking a vacation, a holiday from one form of self-wounding only to wound ourselves again by another means. Taking a vacation from self-wounding raises the question of just how well we actually want to be. The question is humorously asked in the film Annie Hall in which a man goes to a psychiatrist, complaining that his brother in law who lives with him, thinks he is a chicken. 'Describe the symptoms' says the doctor. 'Maybe I can help.' 'Well' replies the man, 'he cackles a lot, he pecks at the carpet and he makes nests in the corners.' The doctor thinks for a moment, then says: 'It sounds like a simple neurosis to me. Bring your brother-in-law in. I think I can cure him completely.' 'Oh no, Doc,' says the man 'we wouldn't want a complete cure, we need the eggs!' That's what happens when we take a vacation approach to self-wounding. We don't ever really commit to being cured or free. We prefer to hang on to our old stuck identity because at least its familiar and more still, in some way or other, it pays off.

Integration

The third response to addictive self-wounding is integration which is all about facing up to the fact that the real is not the ideal but nor does it have to become an ordeal. The surprising thing about integration is that it is often glimpsed before it is thought. Hence the power of films like the Greatest Showman to tell stories in which we recognise our own stories. Or the power of a novel in which we recognise our own struggles being played out. Or when we see something in nature – like the rock wedged between the two cliff faces on the cover of this book - that speaks to our experience. And when we make that journey from dissociation through vacation to integration, we embrace our vulnerability, we bring ourselves out of hiding and we say, first to ourselves and then to the world, 'I am brave, I am bruised, this is who I'm meant to be – this is me.'

For Reflection

Watch or listen to the anthem 'This is Me' from The Greatest Showman[62]. As you do reflect on the fig leaves you use to hide your vulnerability from others.

1. What have you have been told to hide away?

2. What would it take to say 'This is me' as a supervisor?

3. What would it take to enable your supervisees to embrace rather than shun their vulnerabilities?

Chapter Nine
Serial Competence
or Serial Intimacy?

'I've looked at some training programs for leaders [and] I'm discouraged by how often they focus on the development of skills to manipulate the external world rather than the skills necessary to go inward and make the inner journey.'

Parker J. Palmer[63]

The 1997 film Goodwill Hunting tells the story of Will (played by Matt Damon), a young man who has gone off the rails and whose Mathematics teacher tries to get him back on the straight and narrow. The film shows Will being taken to see an Educational Psychologist, then a hypnotherapist and finally, a rather unconventional counsellor played by the actor Robin Williams.

The educational psychologist sits, suited and booted, behind his desk in a study surrounded by the books he has written and read. The hypnotherapist sees Will in a dimly lit room conducive to his modality. Finally, Will is taken to see Robin Williams in a messy room filled to the brim with personal artefacts. This latter session begins with Will walking around the room commenting on what he sees. The conversation establishes that both client and therapist go to the gym and have an interest in keeping fit. But when Will focuses in on a painting of a storm-tossed boat and deduces the therapist's mental state following the recent death of his wife, the session comes to an abrupt end as the counsellor grabs the client by the throat and tells him 'if you ever insult my wife again I will end you'. 'Time up' replies the client.

Each of the three therapeutic approaches are shocking in their own way. Nevertheless, it is much easier to talk about professional distance and the truth that we cannot work with everyone who comes through the consulting room door that it is to take seriously that what the Robin Williams character did was to be utterly authentic, present and vulnerable in the moment and to ask how far we each might go to connect with those who seek us out or are sent to us. Lest I be misunderstood let me be clear that I am not advocating violence in the caring relationship but I am highlighting the truth that not every boundary crossing constitutes a boundary violation. In grabbing the client by the throat, Robin Williams certainly crossed a boundary but as the film goes on to show, it was his willingness to really connect with his client by being authentic in the moment that became the catalyst for the ensuing healing.

In recent years, and in the light of investigations into historic childhood sexual abuse, we have come to know the importance of not touching people wrongly but the longer I practice, and the longer I train others in pastoral care and supervision, the more I worry that in focusing on not touching people *wrongly* we might never get close enough to touching them *rightly*. And I don't just mean physically. I mean going the extra mile to reach people in deeply, authentic, trusting, accountable and committed ways that call us out from behind our professional facades and forge sufficient connectivity without which healing will never happen.

This was brought home to me at the end of a long day of supervising recently. As the day wore on, I became more and more tired and when the last supervisee hadn't arrived five minutes into his allotted time I was more than happy to pack up and go. And so with my coat on and bag packed up I made my way to the door to find him waiting patiently for me and to discover – to my horror – that the door bell was not working.

My heart sank. I wanted to go home. But donning my professional mask once more, I retraced my steps and ushered him into the consulting room. 'I'm so glad to see you' he began 'I've had this really clear sense that I am being invited to practice no longer from competence but from intimacy.' 'Sorry?' I said, taken aback. 'I have this clear sense that I am being invited to practice not so much from competence as from intimacy'.

Now this man is the medical director of a healthcare facility. Competence is what he is trained for. And competence is what he is paid for. 'I have come to realise that competence only takes you so far in professional life; humanity and intimacy are what matters' he continued.

What emerged in the rest of that session was, I hope, of use to my supervisee but what I can say with certainty is that that encounter was one of the most powerful moments of radical mutuality of my entire professional life. As the Buddha is reputed to have said: 'When the pupil is ready the teacher will appear'. I, the supervisor, was that day a pupil. The doctor -my supervisee - was my teacher.

I spend a lot of my time training people to become supervisors. I point them to the books. I set assignments against professional competencies. I teach theory. I introduce them to all sorts of skills for exploring the material that people bring. And ultimately I determine their fitness to practice. But the longer I supervise, the less I trust what passes as 'professional wisdom' and the more I fear that it is really all a defence against vulnerability and an illusory attempt to make us feel that we are in control.

Let me be clear. Training matters! Professional standards matter! Accountability matters! But I no longer believe that supervisees are clamouring for our professional, competent selves so much as longing for professional friends who have befriended their own inner demons, and yet still smile at themselves; people who can get close enough to touch them rightly, rather than remain aloof and distant, ensuring that that we never touch them wrongly.

I have come to the view that those we care for need practitioners whose boundaries are internally rather than externally regulated, practitioners who can trust themselves to get close enough, real enough, honest enough to effect healing rather than to subscribe to the culture of fear; people who can love their clients into wellbeing and not only insure themselves against them.

I worry that with data protection, with professional accreditation and regulation, with the rise in professional practice investigations, performance indicators and the relentless culture of inspection, supervisors are in real danger of throwing the baby out with the bath water in over-valuing competence, undervaluing relationship and valuing mastery (of our discipline) over mystery (in venturing beyond the familiar)[64].

The consequences for training pastoral supervisors are significant. Are we preparing people for a lifetime of serial intimacy or are we simply preparing them for a lifetime of serial competence?[65] If we are only training people to practice from competence, what will they do when their theories no longer support them or help them understand the issues that practice presents? And what will they do when their skill sets no longer plummet the depths to which supervisees require them to go? Furthermore, if supervision training accords competence a value it does not deserve, are we not making it even harder for our students to bring their less than fully competent selves to the table and implicitly encouraging them to hide themselves from being truly seen?

In a very telling sentence, Katherine Mair says that, among her peers who supervise, those who seem to actually help people do so by 'manag[ing] to outgrow the handicaps imposed by their training.'[66] I consider an over-valuing of competence to the neglect of intimacy such a handicap.

Brené Brown describes vulnerability as 'having the courage to show up and be seen when we have no control over the outcome.' I want supervisors who will show up. Not just get their bodies into the room or the bottoms onto the chair, but really show up, courageously present, disarmed not defended. I do not want supervisors to become more objective as if they were blank screens unaffected by what they see and hear. Rather, I want supervisors who can make their subjectivity more available in the service of those who come to them. And I want supervisors who have so befriended themselves that they can go beyond competence to offer intimacy not distance.

And that's why I think the best training and the best Continuous Professional Development for supervisors happens not in conferences or formal workshops, rich though they can be, but in our own homes and offices and care facilities where supervisees, courageously tell the truth about their lives and practice. Because 'when the student (ie supervisor) is ready, then the teacher (in the guise of the supervisee) will most certainly appear.'

For Reflection

Bring to mind the people you supervise.

1. In what ways have they moved you on as a supervisor?

2. In what ways have they invited you to deeper levels of showing up, of presence, of professional courage?

3. Where are you being invited to practice from intimacy and not just competence?

Chapter Ten
From Burnout to Joy at work

*The question is not how to survive, but how to thrive
with passion, compassion, humour and style.*

Maya Angelou

The African-American poet and inspirational writer,
Maya Angelou was a black woman from a poor family.
Maltreated by men; a single mum trying to bring up her
child; turned away because of the colour of her skin from
university; told that she wouldn't amount to much, Maya
Angelou knew the difference between surviving and
thriving long before she formulated the sentence. Born
from hardship, her words have universal and lasting
appeal.

For the last twenty years I have repeated those words 'the
question is not how to survive but how to thrive with
passion, compassion, humour and style' as a mantra each
morning on the way to work. Why? Because I know, only
too well, the struggle some days simply to survive at work
never mind thrive and I know only too well that it doesn't
take much in my working day to kill my passion, drain
my compassion, threaten my humour and eradicate any
traces of style or flair I ever had. And so every morning
for twenty years I have repeated that mantra as I think
about the day ahead, the appointments in my diary, the
people I will be seeing. And as I do, I ask myself what
would it take to turn surviving into thriving today, not in
some airy-fairy pie in the sky way but as I look ahead to
that meeting I've got at 11am, how could I thrive and help
others thrive in that meeting rather than just survive, and

when I look at that person I really would rather not have to see at 1230 how could I help us both get beyond surviving to thriving? The truth is that some days I manage it better than other days. And some days I don't manage it at all. I first came across Maya Angelou at a time in my life when I was completely burnt out and needed to take four months off work just to recover.

Emotional Exhaustion: First sign of burnout
It was in the early 1990s. I was living in London and working as a chaplain in an AIDS hospice in the early days of HIV long before the advent of retroviral drugs when the gap between diagnosis and death was often as short as three months. In the summer of 1994, I buried someone in their twenties every day for twenty eight days in succession. And what's more I had the bizarre experience of having people come up to me at the end of a friend's funeral to book me for their own funeral the way an engaged couple might go to other people's weddings in the hope of finding a band for their forthcoming wedding. By the end of August 1994, I was wrung out, exhausted and numbed by the bucket loads of pain I had accumulated over the years. Little did I know then that emotional exhaustion was the first indicator of burnout and I was already travelling at speed down the road to my own ruin.

Depersonalisation: Second sign of burnout
The second sign of burnout is depersonalisation which, with the benefit of hindsight, I now recognise I was experiencing. The more need I saw, the more I wanted to run away from it and hide. The problem was not that I did not care. Quite the opposite. The problem was that I cared so much I couldn't bear it anymore. And so I began to

make myself or the people I cared for invisible or at least blurry and out of focus. Some days I could fake it but other days I literally hid: in the sluice room; in the toilet, behind the closed door of my office with an engaged sign on the door, ignoring the phone, my head in my hands, wondering who cares for the carer who cannot even care for himself? Of course, I never told anyone about that but years later, I recognised myself in a wonderful book called *Care Giver Stress and Staff Support* in which Irene Renzenbrink talks about how, in our attempts to survive the costs of caring for others, we build fortresses around ourselves to protect ourselves from being overwhelmed: She writes:

> We add a moat, we throw in some crocodiles ... we build higher and higher walls. Sooner or later, we find ourselves locked in by the very defences we have constructed for our own protection. We will find the key to our liberation only when we accept that what we once did to survive is now destroying us.[67]

Over the years I have experimented with a variety of moats and crocodiles to make myself unavailable and unreachable when feeling stressed and I have observed many colleagues and managers doing the same: carrying a folder and walking at speed down a hospital corridor; cutting off conversations when I don't want to engage with a sudden 'must dash'; responding to emails with the words 'in haste' when I cannot be bothered engaging more fully. As temporary survival techniques they have their uses, but as habitual practices to get me through the next decade until I can retire they will never bring joy or wellbeing.

Helplessness: Third sign of burnout
The third sign of burnout is an overwhelming sense of helplessness, of being utterly defeated and unable to make a difference. No matter what I did as a hospice chaplain, patients still died. No matter how well I counselled their relatives and friends, grief and deep sadness inevitably followed. But what turned that experience into burnout for me was the cancerous, corrosive thinking that plagues so many wholehearted practitioners. It all starts fairly innocuously by saying 'I don't have enough resources' to meet the needs of all the people in my care, but then slips into saying 'I can't do enough' which, in turn, opens the door to self-accusation: 'if only I was bigger, brighter, more broad shouldered', 'if only I worked harder, stayed later, squeezed even more into an overly long day' then I could make things better for the folk I care for. This kind of thinking leads to the final defeatist statement of all: 'Its not that I don't have enough resources, its not that I cannot do enough because I am so limited, the root problem is with me, in that *I* am not enough.' And with that kind of toxic thinking, the three hallmarks of burnout: exhaustion, depersonalization and that all-pervading sense of personal and professional inadequacy all took their toll and five hundred plus deaths later I ended up traumatised by the very trauma in which I was immersed. I could no longer function and ended up off work for four months costing the taxpayer and the health service an awful lot of money.

That experience from twenty plus years ago was what led me into psychotherapy in the first place and laid the foundation for a lifetime of working in the field of staff support and wellbeing. But since that episode of burnout there have been a few near misses over the years. Like so many in the caring professions, I started out with a fire in my belly. I did my training, studied hard and was eager to make a difference. I had been inspired by excellent teachers and supported by work-based supervisors who believed in me and nurtured my passion. And after a break in academia to heal and recover, I went back to hospice care to do what I know and love best: getting real with people who are in the business of shedding their masks, telling the truth about their lives and knowing the sheer freedom and joy that comes when the games have stopped.

But ten years later the tell-tale signs were returning. I loved the patients. I was getting on well with my colleagues. The job was hard work but very fulfilling but there was something about the increasingly aggressive management style of the hospice which jarred with everything I stood for. Person-centred care was what I was asked (and indeed wanted) to deliver but the directive to deliver it came from a manager who did not leave many of us staff feeling that we too were persons. Ironically the hospice motto was 'Making every minute count' but in practice, staff were increasingly directed away from the very people whose clocks were ticking - the dying – to spend more and more time away in paperwork or in front of computer screens. As a result, values and policies that looked great on paper were becoming adrift from work place reality and staff morale was at an all-time low. Once again I was sinking. Once again I was feeling helpless and inadequate to make a difference. But then a strange thing happened which opened my eyes.

My epiphany did not happen at a professional development workshop or even in supervision. It happened in a mandatory health and safety session that hospice staff were obliged to attend each year. This particular session on fire training began with the trainer filling six large metal bins with highly flammable material and setting each ablaze. Within seconds the flames were leaping over the edge. He then handed each member of staff a fire extinguisher and taught us how to train the hose at the very heart of the fire. In less than three seconds the leaping flames were completely extinguished and all that was left was smoke and ashes. And in a split second I recognised something I had seen throughout my working life: fires in the bellies of highly committed staff extinguished by policies or protocols, back biting or bitching until the very thing that once fired them up and got them out of bed in the morning to come to work is hosed down, extinguished and reduced to dust and ashes.

My protest is not against policies or protocols, nor is it directed against our organizational leaders. My protest is against behaviours, environments and working practices that extinguish the fire in the bellies of committed, wholehearted staff when mission statements and corporate values are used as sticks to beat them rather than as dynamic energies which pervade the culture and ethos of the whole organization and which are modelled by those in leadership positions. Fire can scorch and singe and burn but it can also warm and heat and light. And it can be extinguished in three seconds by a look or a word, by the wagging of a finger, the apportioning of blame and by practices that value systems more highly than humans. The exponential rise in professional conversations about resilience is living proof that many practitioners are struggling to keep their inner motivational pilot lights lit (never mind stoking the fire in their bellies) and that too many are sick and tired of being hosed down by policies and performance indicators that extinguish the joy they once knew at work.

During the second world war, a series of three posters were commissioned and printed to help boost morale in the UK. The first poster ran: *'Your courage, Your cheerfulness, Your resolution Will bring Us Victory.'* One simple message in ten words. The second poster, which also used ten words, was released a few years further into the war: *'Freedom is in peril. Defend it with all your might'*. The third piece of propaganda was held under wraps. Two and a half million posters were printed but strict instructions were issued that it was only to be used in the most extreme of extreme circumstances should Germany ever invade Britain. And this time the poster had only five words. *'Keep Calm And Carry On'*. How ironic that this message, intended only to be used in times of utter and unthinkable extremity, has become so commonplace today on posters and mugs and T shirts: a message from a time of war and unrest, that speaks to so many today in a time of supposed peace and stability.

Personally, I think the call to show courage, cheerfulness and resolution (poster one) or to defend everything that the caring professions stand for (poster two) is wearing thin and lays the shoulder of responsibility too heavily on front line staff. But I also wonder just how long we are going to be able to keep calm and carry on with so many of our institutions and organisations on their knees.

That third war time poster has spawned many a spoof a great deal of which are not suitable to be seen in polite company. But if I was to design a mug that supervisors might use to promote resilience in the workplace it would be something along the lines of: 'Stand up and be heard!'; 'Wake up and do something'; or 'Enough is enough is enough!' because there comes a time when keeping calm is *not* enough and when patching people up and sending them back to their soul extinguishing workplaces is not an ethical option. Of course, supervisors are in the business of fostering resilience but I think we need to be very careful that in doing so we do not become pawns in an organisational game. 'Fiona isn't very resilient. Let's send her to supervision.' 'Donald has been through a rough patch. A good dose of supervision would soon build him up again.'

I have a deep suspicion that, underlying conversations about resilience in many organisations is a belief that the problem lies with individuals and not with systems. Wellbeing studies are to be welcomed but we should be on the lookout for just how commonplace it has become to read report after report which focuses on 'a lack of resilience in the workforce' rather than on the myriad of symptoms of chronic ill health within organisations themselves.

I am deeply concerned that pastoral supervision runs the risk of becoming the latest form of self-medication for organisations suffering from chronic institutional anxiety. Traditional understandings of supervision envisage the supervisor asking the supervisee 'how can I help you survive in your toxic environment?' but as we revisit and revision pastoral supervision I think the time has come for supervisors to widen the lens of our care and ask 'how can we together resist and transform those toxic environments?' And so the time has come to not only ask how we supervisors are fostering resilience but, more pertinently, how we are fostering resistance.

In the 1980's the social psychotherapy movement asked: 'How many battered wives does a counsellor need to see before she realises that something needs to be done about the men who are battering them?' In the same vein, forty years on, the question has now become: 'how many battered and bruised practitioners whose souls are on life support in toxic contexts do pastoral supervisors have to see before we speak out and challenge the institutions that are causing such serious work based injuries?'

Many of the supervisees I support have lived with personal and organizational exhaustion for long enough. They are sick and tired of their institutions responding to every crisis by simply issuing new rules and compliance demands and they are tired of the paperwork which keeps them away from human contact. The NHS staff I support are bone weary of the intense and never ending media scrutiny they are subjected to in the Press and feel starved by the resource rationing which comes from organisations knowing the price of everything and the value of nothing. The time has come to turn weariness, low morale, lost energy and sheer frustration into constructive impatience and do something new; not write another report, not throw money on another short lived flashy initiative, but do something fresh that converts the moaning and groaning, the bitching and the cynicism that many of us experience at work, into something constructive – something which releases rather than zaps us of energy.

What Robin Meyers says about the church has wider relevance here.

> [the church] keeps trying to repair itself by remodelling – doctrinally, aesthetically or programmatically – but it seems to have forgotten how to resist. In addition to all the duties of ministry .. we are called to embody resistance to all that is false. We are called to resist with mind, soul and body all that masquerades as truth. We must push back against the destructions and mythologies of the marketplace, the cruel panacea of take-this-pill medicine and the bankrupt Wall Street bargain that places private ambition over intimacy and stock portfolios over people.'[68]

Constructive impatience says that at any given moment, each one of us has the power to say: this is not how the story is going to end. Constructive impatience says that with courage, change can happen. And what are supervisors if not agents of change?

For Reflection

As a supervisee

1. what dampens down your aspirations or extinguishes your hope at work?

2. What ignites you and keeps your inner pilot light flickering?

As a supervisor

1. how do you collude with the status quo?

2. How do you foster resistance in your supervisees?

Chapter Eleven
Supervision and Transformation

Wherever we are, we are at a perimeter.
At the heart of the most familiar,
we are at the edge.
Whatever we do or think or feel,
we are on a ledge poised above the darkness:
an extinction or an epiphany
that makes or remakes us,
on the other side of the event.

Whatever we are, whatever we do,
ruler or ruled, consumer or consumed,
we are always on the line
where there's always the possibility
of a sudden or an unheralded dawn.
It may not happen today or tomorrow or soon;
but it will happen.

Janes Gleeson[69]

Often when I am delivering training or facilitating professional development workshops I use short film clips. One of my favourites is a ninety second advert for Nolan's Cheddar made for Irish television. The clip opens with a mouse emerging from a hole in the skirting board approaching a mouse trap on which some cheese has been strategically placed. After a few nibbles the inevitable happens, the trap is released and the mouse finds himself belly up struggling to survive. To everyone's surprise what happens next is startling: the mouse turns the trap into a rowing machine and builds up his muscles ready for an escape. I show that film for three reasons.

The first is that it succinctly depicts the reason why many a person ends up in pastoral supervision in the first place. Like the mouse they were getting on with their life, going about their professional business and doing what they do best until, wham, bham it all goes wrong and they find themselves caught in a vice, trapped, ensnared and struggling for survival. The clip underlines the truth that a lot of supervision 'begins from the ragged edges of pain.'[70]

The second reason I show that clip is that it neatly portrays an understanding of pastoral supervision which is prevalent at the moment, not least among our churches. The view of supervision as a kind of gym or rehab centre in which personal trainers (known as supervisors) help supervisees recover from work or ministry acquired injuries.

And the third reason I show that clip is because understandings of supervision as recovery from professional injury, a means of personal survival and as opportunities for fostering resilience are now rightly being challenged by understandings of supervision as a catalyst for the transformation of those work settings and cultures which leave staff injured in the first place. And this is where revisiting and revisioning comes in.

Supervision and the Human Life Cycle
Walter Brueggemann, a contemporary American biblical scholar, brilliantly connects the development of the Hebrew Scriptures[71] (the Law, the Prophets and the Wisdom writings) with the human life cycle.[72] He says that the Torah or Law, the first five books, corresponds to

the first half of life. This is the period in which we need structures, traditions and a certain amount of predictability and stability to grow up and find our identity. What he is talking about corresponds – broadly speaking - to the normative dimension of supervision.[73] And this is the stage that many of our caring agencies are working so hard at

- complying with professional standards;
- establishing regulatory bodies
- drawing up codes of ethics;
- implementing ways that make vulnerable people rather than organizational reputation central in how we go about our business etc
- requiring carers to engage in regular supervision.

In the last ten years since the founding of APSE (the regulatory body for pastoral supervision in the UK) churches and voluntary agencies have worked hard at becoming mainstream, of gaining professional trust and of being accepted as accountable and transparent. But I wonder if what we have done mirrors what gay people do when they are in the closet; playing straight in the hope that we will fit in and be accepted by whoever we think counts while perfecting the art of ventriloquism – speaking the way other professionals speak – in order to be heard and taken seriously. Sadly, the very promotion of pastoral supervision as normative - as a requirement of professional life rather than as something to opt into - presents the biggest threat to the future of supervision we have seen in the last decade. Dip into the literature and you will find supervision referred to as 'snoopervision';[74] 'big brother watching over my shoulder'; a form of 'scrutiny and quality control'. Increasingly people write of supervision as 'yet another technology of surveillance'[75] and a way in which organisations 'manage risk adversity'.[76]

In my own practice over the last ten years, what I have sadly seen too often are more supervisees than ever coming because they *have to* rather than because they *want to;* attending rather than engaging; complying rather than enquiring and reporting rather than reflecting. All of which makes me wonder whether the time has come for supervision that can truly be called *pastoral* to come out of the closet and admit that it is not actually straight or mainstream after all; not just a bells and smells version of something that other professions do but in fact something diverse and queer, practiced by some diverse and queer people who march to the sound of a different drum, a different set of values, a different take on what it means to be human and on what it means to flourish and to fall.

The Prophets
According to Brueggemann, the prophets initiate us into adulthood by moving us beyond rule keeping and externalised sources of authority (which are so necessary in the first normative stage of our lives) to healthy self-criticism and critically re-evaluating things in the second stage of our lives. The supervision tradition that has been passed down to us by social workers, counsellors and educationalists has taught us to value the restorative dimension of supervision, which Sheila Ryan calls 'supervision as compassionate medicine'.[77] The need for compassionate medicine is something we all need from time to time and is often the pivotal hinge that swings someone who pitches up in supervision because they *have to* into someone who pitches up because they *want to.* But

who is this compassionate medicine for? The injured mouse ie the supervisee - or the professional system to which the mouse will return? At its simplest, prophetic critique asks this very challenging question:

> Is it ethical to simply patch supervisees up and send them back to the soul destroying contexts in which they work while doing and saying nothing to change those contexts?

And this is where prophetic understandings of what we mean by pastoral come in.

Pastoral as responding to need
In 1964 Clebsch & Jaekle defined pastoral as 'helping acts directed towards the healing, sustaining, guiding and reconciling of troubled persons.'[78] That understanding of fixing broken people is very much around and has dominated people's mindsets for generations but it should be noted that it is a deficit model which, by its very nature means you have to be in some kind of need or you have to be troubled to access pastoral care. Which raises the question: where is the pastoral care of people who are happy? Where is the pastoral care of those who have gone beyond surviving and are actually thriving?

The dominant deficit understanding of 'pastoral' began to shift by the turn of the millennium, when pastoral theologians like Emmanuel Lartey widened the narrow lens which saw pastoral as fixing broken individuals and re-visioned *pastoral* as fostering 'holistic communities in which people may live humane lives' Lartey 2003. And this is where I welcome the push that the Australian Royal Commission and the past cases reviews in the UK into child sexual abuse have given us in asking us not just to root out the abusers but to foster 'holistic communities in which people may live humane lives.'[79] Feminist pastoral theologian Bonnie Miller-McLemore tells us how:

> By breaking silences and speaking out against anything that impedes human flourishing; by speaking truth to power and by empowering people to rise up against whatever holds them down.[80]

What Lartey and Miller-McLemore are pointing to is nothing less than a recovery of the biblical prophetic tradition which continuously reminds us that the journey is from I to We, from exclusion to inclusion and from isolation to being in community. The Christian writer Bradford Littlejohn puts it this way:

> 'We live our lives between the twin poles of Incarnation and Resurrection. Incarnation invites us to engage with the world. Resurrection requires us to transform it.' [81]

The point he is making is that to engage with the world is to say that matter matters whereas to work for the world's transformation is to affirm that because matter matters, it is incumbent on us who supervise to do whatever we can to not only promote the health and wellbeing of our supervisees but also the health and wellbeing of the contexts and systems within which they work. And so, prophetic critique asks whether those of who supervise are willing to own the *pastoral* in our identity and balance restoration of individuals with transformation of contexts? Traditional understandings of the restorative dimension of supervision ask 'how can I help you survive in your toxic environment?' Prophetic critique asks 'how can we together resist and transform those toxic environments?'

Prophets never were easy people to be around and their challenges never were particularly palatable. Most supervisors are doing their very best to manage the demands of serial intimacy. The thought that they might be called to intentionally engage with – rather than just hear about – their supervisees' messy contexts, is likely to leave a lot of them uncomfortable since the task seems so daunting. Two pieces of Rabbinical wisdom offer a way forward.

> If you see what needs to be repaired and how to repair it then you have found a piece of the world that God has left for you to complete. But if you only see what is wrong and what is ugly, it is you yourself that needs repair.[82]

> You are not obligated to complete the work but neither are you free to abandon it.[83]

Experiment

Whether working with an individual, a team or a group, one place to begin on the road to transformation lies in exploiting the experimental opportunities that supervision presents. Within the safety of a room, where the door is shut and there are no CCTV cameras, supervisors can experiment in all sorts of ways such as by asking a supervisee, what they would like to say to the organisation they work for, if they did not have to worry about putting their job at risk or to couch things in polite language?[84] And then having heard the raw, unedited version (which may be rather colourful) ask the supervisee what the ethical and professional translation of those raw comments might be. Being able to discharge raw feeling and emotion in supervision and then to build a bridge from that back to realistic transformative action are invaluable facets of supervision.

Another powerful way of accessing supervisees' relationships with their work context is for the supervisor to ask the supervisee what would happen if they and key players from the organisation they are struggling with were to be cast away together on a desert island with no means of escape.[85] Faced with that question, many supervisees have said that they would rather throw themselves to the sharks than cohabit the island with their managers or CEOs! Whatever we do, for most of us, speaking truth to power is a risky business which brings up all sorts of levels of anxiety. And that's why I am increasingly convinced of the need to counter the isolation, the anxiety and the sheer terror of standing up to those who have power over of us by fostering resilience and resistance through group and not only individual supervision. Because what working in a group does is to boldly assert that together we can build bridges from passivity to agency, from disempowerment to empowerment and from defeat to action.

I know only too well how fearful many supervisors are of running group supervision but many of those fears stem from uncritically buying into a therapeutic paradigm which tells us that we need to understand what is going on and know a lot about group dynamics to facilitate groups safely. But if we revise our notions of supervisor as expert to supervisor as facilitator [ie the move from conceiving the supervisor as sage on the stage to guide by our side] then with a healthy dose of courage and an awareness of Lencioni's five dimensions of group life[86] (outlined in Chapter Six) we can go a long way in enabling contextually sensitive, transformative pastoral supervision.

Wisdom

According to Walter Brueggemann, going beyond the expected, the conventional, the routine are all hallmarks of the Wisdom Literature, the third literary category of the Hebrew Bible, in which Wisdom is portrayed as the capacity to sift what we have received and experienced and to embrace what seems apparently contradictory in ourselves and in others. Brueggemann sees this as the task of the second half of life which I reckon is not so much marked by the accumulation of years as it is by the evacuation of fears; that stage in life when our locus of validation becomes far more internal than external and when we own what we do as supervisors rather than feel the need to justify it to others.

It takes guts to go beyond doing what our supervisory elders told us to do, to uncritically accept what they published and to re-evaluate their legacies. But to refuse to do so is to make yesterday rather than tomorrow our permanent address[87] and to lock ourselves into repeating the past rather than risking new futures. Following Noel Davis's invitation, we who supervise will know we are living in an age of wisdom when we venture beyond the familiar in our practice, range wider than routine in our interactions, delve beneath the old certainties, break from the programmed and regularly find ourselves and those we supervise taking different ways home.[88]

For Reflection

1. To what extent do you find yourself fostering resilience and / or fostering resistance in your supervisees?

2. What use do you make of supervision as a place of experimentation in which supervisees can rehearse strategies, conversations, and interactions geared towards identifying unhelpful organisational or interpersonal behaviours in the workplace?

3. As a supervisor, what from your training or professional formation no longer serves you and what is worth preserving?

4. What are your sources of wisdom and ongoing nurture as a supervisor? Ted Talks? CPD events? Regarding your supervisees as teachers?

Epilogue

Paradigm shifts in Pastoral Supervision

The biggest changes we have seen in the field of pastoral supervision in the last ten years are tabled below.

Paradigm Shifts in Pastoral Supervision	
From	*To*
Supervision *of* Pastoral Work	A pastoral attitude to supervision
Supervising a pastoral worker	Attending to systemic wellbeing
Single lens supervision	Variofocal supervision
Single modality exploration	Multimodal exploration
Supervision as expert (locus of expertise in knowledge domain)	Supervisors as facilitator of inquiry (locus of expertise in domain of reflection)
Uni-professional supervision	Cross-professional supervision

The shift from pastoral supervision understood as the supervision of pastoral workers who do pastoral things to an attitudinal commitment to seeing things wholistically and working for the wellbeing of all dimensions of the system (individual, team and organizational wellbeing) marks the biggest shift in understanding the emerging discipline of pastoral supervision.

A second shift is from supervisors looking at everything through one single lens (the pirate syndrome) to supervisors utilising a whole range of lenses (diagnostic; solution focused; interpretative; identity; imaginative etc) according to the supervisee's need and developmental stage.

A third shift is from a single modality approach to supervision ('this is me and this is how I supervise') to a more nuanced and multimodal approach which asks 'how can I attune my approach to meet your personality and your ways of processing as we explore what you are bringing to supervision today?'

Underpinning a varifocal and multimodal approach is a further shift away from the supervisor as expert whose effectiveness rests on what they know[89] (the knowledge domain) to supervisor as facilitator of inquiry whose effectiveness rests on their ability to foster reflective exploration.[90]

The relocation of expertise from knowledge in the field to facilitating inquiry characterises the fifth shift which is from uni-professional supervision (in which the supervisor works in same field as the supervisee) to cross-professional supervision in which the capacity to facilitate reflection is more important than insider knowledge.

Of course, not everyone has welcomed these changes and not all our supervisors have the skills, training or self-restraint necessary to facilitate inquiry rather than to practice from a place of knowing and experience gained over years working in the same field.[91] But I think, at root, the biggest resistance to re-visioning pastoral supervision as a cross-professional discipline arises from the prevailing belief that supervisors feel that they need to understand in order to best help. And cross-professional pastoral supervision simply says that that is simply not true. In the story we heard in Chapter Three about Fiona, the manager of the Dementia Care Facility, it would not have mattered whether her supervisor also worked in that professional arena since she was not looking to be understood. Nor would it have mattered if Fiona's supervisor had a psychotherapeutic training which equipped her with insights into why she was experiencing life as she was, since she was not looking for her supervisor to interpret her. What mattered for Fiona – and indeed for most supervisees post training – is that they are trusted as the experts in their own story and that supervisors know how to elicit and harness their reflexive curiosity until they regain access to whatever aspect of wisdom is temporarily out of their reach. And when supervisors do that, then supervision is truly pastoral both for supervisees and for those they serve.

1. What for you makes supervision 'pastoral'?

2. Which lenses do you regularly employ when supervising, and which remain underdeveloped?

3. What is your default supervisory modality? Thinking of your supervisees, might other modalities also serve their needs?

4. How open are you to supervising those who work in professional disciplines with which you are not familiar?

5. Do you see yourself as supervising people's work or supervising people who do the work?

End Notes

[1] David Whyte (2001) Crossing the Unknown Sea: Work as a Pilgrimage of Identity, Riverhead.

[2] Jochen Encke (2008) 'Breaking the Box: Supervision — A challenge to free ourselves' in Shohet, R (ed.) 2008, Passionate Supervision, London: Jessica Kingsley, 16-32.

[3] Sheila Ryan (2004) Vital Practice: stories from the healing arts, the homeopathic and supervisory way, Portland: Sea Change, 4.

[4] cf Rita Irwin and Alex de Cosson (2004) A/r/tography: Rendering self through arts-based living inquiry. Vancouver: Pacific Educational Press.

5 Gloria Anzaldúa, (1987), Borderlands, Anzaldúa lived her whole life in the in-between places of geography, race, language, colour, belief and sexuality. She was born and raised on the Texas/Mexico border.

6 Parker J. Palmer, (2004) A Hidden Wholeness: The Journey Toward an Undivided Life, Jossey-Bass, San Francisco, CA.

[7] T S Eliot, Four Quartets, Burnt Norton.

[8] Nicki Weld,(2012) A practical guide to transformative supervision for the helping professions: Amplifying insight, London: Jessica Kingsley.

[9] Allyson Davys and Liz Beddoe (2010), Best Practice in Professional Supervision: A Guide for the Helping Professions. London and Philadelphia : Jessica Kingsley Publishers, 81.

[10] Donald Schon (1985) The Reflective Practitioner: How professionals think in action. New York: Basic Books.

[11] Nicki Weld (2012) A practical guide to transformative supervision for the helping professions: Amplifying insight, London: Jessica Kingsley, 25.

[12] Noel Davis (2011) Together at the Edge: Trust Me, Narooma, NSW: Lifeflow Education.

[13] I wrote this alternative to capture the stark contrasts between Noel Davis's poem and my experience.

[14] Robin Shohet (ed.) 2011 *Supervision as transformation: A passion for learning,* London and Philadelphia: Jessica Kingsley, 10.

[14] Nicki Weld (2012) A practical guide to transformative supervision for the helping professions: Amplifying insight, London: Jessica Kingsley, 25.

[14] Noel Davis (2011) *Together at the Edge: Trust Me,* Narooma, NSW: Lifeflow Education.

[14] I wrote this alternative to capture the stark contrasts between Noel David's poem and my experience.

[14] Robin Shohet (ed.) 2011 op.cit.

[15] Allyson Davys and Liz Beddoe (2010), *Best Practice in Professional Supervision: A Guide for the Helping Professions.* London and Philadelphia : Jessica Kingsley Publishers 87.

[16] Davys and Beddoe op. cit. 87.

[17] Jane Leach and Michael Paterson (2015), *Pastoral Supervision: A Handbook, Second Edition*, London: SCM; Paterson and Rose (2014*) Enriching Ministry: Pastoral Supervision in Context*, London: SCM; Helen Dixon Cameron,(2018) *Living in the Gaze of God: Supervision and Ministerial Flourishing,* Norwich: SCM

[18] Michael Paterson, 2016.

[19] Mark Manson (2016) The Subtle art of not giving a F*CK: A Counterintuitive Approach to Living a Good Life, New York:HarperOne.

[20] I have been unable to trace the origins of this saying.

[21] Mezirow calls these 'disorienting dilemmas' cf Jack Mezirow (2000). 'Learning to think like an adult: core concepts of transformation theory', in Mezirow, J. & Associates (eds*.), Learning as transformation: critical perspectives on a theory in progress*, San Francisco: Jossey-Bass.

[22] Joseph Sittler (1986) *Gravity and Grace: Reflections and Provocations*, Minneapolis: Augsburg Publishing House, 1.

[23] Joan Wilmot in Shohet, R. (ed.) 2011 *Supervision as transformation: A passion for learning,* London and Philadelphia: Jessica Kingsley, 69.

[24] Kenneth Pohly (1977) *Pastoral Supervision: Inquiries into Pastoral Care,* Houston, Texas: Institute of Religion later revised and published in 2001 as *Transforming the Rough Places: The Ministry of Supervision,* Dayton, Ohio: Whaleprints.

[25] This fictitious supervision scenario was written by Michael Paterson for training purposes.

[26] This chapter was inspired by the ground breaking doctoral research of Dr Neil Millar, Canberra, Australia. I am indebted to Neil for permission to revision his findings.

[27] Richard Bandler and John Grindler (1982) *Reframing: Neurolinguistic Programming and the Transformation of Meaning*, Utah: Real People Press, 1.

[28] Bandler and Grindler op. cit.

[29] Renee Swope, www.reneeswope.com accessed 26 February 2020.

[30] 'We are called into healing not curing' Rachel Held Evans (2015) *Searching for Sunday: Loving, Leaving and Finding the Church*, Nashville, Tennesee: Thomas Nelson, 208

[31] This approach is exemplified in Noble, Gray and Johnston, (2016) *Critical Supervision for the Human Services: A Social Model to Promote Learning and Value-based Practice*. London: Jessica Kingsley Publishers.

[32] Examples include Parker J. Palmer (1999) *Let your Life Speak: Listening for the Voice of Vocation*, New York: JosseyBass; Ewan Kelly (2012) *Personhood and Presence: Self as a resource for spiritual and pastoral care*, London: Continuum; Val Wosket (1999), *The therapeutic use of self: Counselling practice, research and supervision,* London: Routledge.

[33] John Patton (2012) 'Embodying Wisdom: Pastoral Proverbs for Reflective Practice', *Reflective Practice: Formation and Supervision in Ministry*, Vol. 32, 136.

[34] David Whyte (2011) *Crossing the Unknown Sea – Work as a Pilgrimage of Identity*, New York: Riverhead Books.

[35] Cf *The Complete Poems of Emily Dickinson* Edited by Mabel Loomis Todd and T.W. Higginson.

[36] Examples include Gillie Bolton (2005) *Reflective Practice: Writing and Professional Development*, 2nd edition, London: Sage; Nicki Weld (2012) *A practical guide to transformative supervision for the helping professions: Amplifying insight,* London: Jessica Kingsley; and Anna Chesner and Lia Zografou (2013) *Creative Supervision Across Modalities*, London: Jessica Kingsley.

[37] John Patton (2012) 'Embodying Wisdom: Pastoral Proverbs for Reflective Practice', *Reflective Practice: Formation and Supervision in Ministry*, Vol. 32, 136.

[38] A term used by George Mackay Brown in his poem 'What is an Orcadian?' in Maggie Fergusson (2006) *George Mackay Brown: The Life.* London: John Murray.

[39] Michael Paterson

[40] Michael Paterson

[41] Michael Paterson

[42] "Vulnerability is not winning or losing; it's having the courage to show up and be seen when we have no control over the outcome. Vulnerability is not weakness; it's our greatest measure of courage." Brené Brown (2015) *Rising Strong*, London: Penguin.

[43] Lencioni (2002) *The Five Dysfunctions of a Team,* Place: San Francisco: JosseyBass. In my adaptation of Lencioni I have modified his second rung 'conflict' to 'difference' since experience has taught me that when differences are acknowledged and embraced (rather than swept under the carpet) the likelihood of conflict is lessened.

[44] Audre Lorde (1984) 'Poetry is Not a Luxury', *Sister Outsider: Essays and Speeches*, Berkeley, California: Ten Speed Press.

[45] cf Darren Fleming, 2018, *Don't be a Dick: Creating Connections that make Influence Happen,*

DarrenFleming.com.au, 19.

[46] Parker J. Palmer www.CourageRenewal.org accessed 1 March 2020

[47] Lorde, Audre. 1984. *Sister Outsider: Essays and Speeches* . Berkeley, CA: Crossing Press, 18.

[48] Lorde, op. cit.

[49] Steve Page and Val Wosket (1994) *Supervising the Counsellor. A Cyclical Model*, London: Routledge.

[50] Parker J. Palmer (1993) *To Know as We are Known: A spirituality of Education*, San Francisco: Harper One, 71-75.

[51] Re pitching interventions to meet supervisees' stages of development see Jane Leach and Michael Paterson, *Pastoral Supervision: A Handbook*, 2nd Edition, London: SCM, 131-138.

[52] Antony Williams (1995) *Visual and Active Supervision: Roles, Focus, Technique*, New York, London: Norton.

[53] op. cit.

[54] cf Rumi's poem 'The Guest House' in which he compares being human to being a guest house with unexpected visitors who bring surprises! Jalaluddin Rumi (2004) *This being human is a guest house*, trans Coleman Barks with John Moynce, A. J. Arberry, London: Penguin.

[55] Brené Brown (2015) *Rising Strong*, London: Penguin.

[56] Janet Morley, (2006) *All Desires Known,* 3rd ed. Harrisburg, Pennsylvania: Morehouse.

[57] The story is told in the New Testament Gospel of Matthew 2:16-18

[58] The song was written by Justin Paul and Benj Pasek. © Sony/ATV Music Publishing LLC, Kobalt Music Publishing Ltd.

[59] https://themindsjournal.com/tag/katherine-mckennitt accessed 28 February 2020

[60] Michael Paterson

[61] cf Anthem 'This is Me' from *The Greatest Showman* written by Justin Paul and Benj Pasek. © Sony/ATV Music Publishing LLC, Kobalt Music Publishing Ltd.

[62] https://www.youtube.com/watch?v=wEJd2RyGm8Q Accessed 28 February 2020

[63] Parker J. Palmer (2003) 'Teaching with heart and soul: Reflections on spirituality in teacher education', *Journal of Teacher Education*, 54 (5) 376–85.

[64] Noel Davis op. cit.

[65] What Derek Fraser, one of the founding Fathers of APSE says of healthcare chaplains can also be said of pastoral supervisors: 'Who else, with nothing in their hands, deals daily with the bruised, the battered and the defeated?' That is what practicing from intimacy looks like.

[66] Katherine Mair cited in Val Wosket (1999), *The therapeutic use of self: Counselling practice, Research and Supervision,* London: Routledge, 133

[67] Irene Renzenbrink (2011) *Caregiver Stress and Staff Support in Illness, Dying and Bereavement*, Oxford, Oxford University Press, 43-4.

[68] Robin Meyers (2015), *Spiritual Defiance: Building a Beloved Community of Resistance,* New Haven, Connecticut.: Yale University Press, 18.

[69] James Gleeson, 'Along the fault line. Late slippages and abrasions', Unpublished Manuscript. Gleeson (1915-2002) was Australia's foremost surrealist artist. .

[70] Ian Morgan Cron, (2013), *Chasing Francis: A Pilgrim's Tale*, Grand Rapids, Michigan: Zondervan. Cron writes: 'all ministry begins at the ragged edges of our own pain'.

[71] Often referred to as the *Old Testament* by Christians

[72] See Walter Brueggemann and Tod Linafelt (2012), *An Introduction to the Old Testament: The Canon and Christian Imagination*, 2nd ed. Westminster John Knox Press.

[73] Fancesca Inskipp and Brigid Proctor identified three tasks in supervision. The normative tasks which deals with managerial concerns; the formative

task which fosters growth and development in the supervisee and the restorative task which offers the opportunity to discharge feelings and recover confidence and courage. Cf Inskipp & Proctor (1993) *The Art, Craft and Tasks of Counselling Supervision*, London: Cascade.

[74] Oversight deemed to be excessively invasive or prying.

[75] T Gilbert (2001) 'Reflective Practice and Clinical Supervision: Meticulous Rituals of the Confessional', *Journal of Advanced Nursing*, 36(2) 199-205.

[76] Nicki Weld (2012) *A practical guide to transformative supervision for the helping professions: Amplifying insight*, London: Jessica Kingsley, 22.

[77] Sheila Ryan (2004) *Vital Practice: stories from the healing arts, the homeopathic and supervisory way*, Portland: Sea Change, 106.

[78] Cf William A. Clebsch (1964) *Pastoral Care in Historical Perspective:* An Essay with Exhibits, Harper Torchbooks.

[79] Emmanuel Lartey (2003) *In Living Colour: An Intercultural Approach to Pastoral Care and Counselling*. London: Jessica Kingsley.

[80] Bonnie Miller-McLemore, (2012) *Christian Theology in Practice: Discovering a Discipline*, Grand Rapids, MI: Eerdmans.

[81] W. Bradford Littlejohn (2009) *The Mercersburg Theology and the Quest for Reformed Catholicity*, Oregon: Pickwick.

[82] Cf Samuel Heilman, Menachem Friedman (2010) *The Rebbe: The Life and Afterlife of Menachem Mendel Schneerson*, New Jersey: Princeton University Press.

[83] Rabbi Tareon, *Tikun Olam*.

[84] cf Peter Hawkins and Robin Shohet (2012) *Supervising in the Helping Professions*, (4th Edn.), Maidenhead: OUP.

[85] cf Hawkins and Shohet op. cit.

[86] Building trust; embracing differences; fostering commitment; encouraging accountability; working towards an agreed goal. cf Lencioni (2002) *The Five Dysfunctions of a Team*, Place: San Francisco: JosseyBass.

[87] e.e.cummings, (1923) *Complete Poems; 1904-1962*, New York: Liveright. 'Tomorrow is our permanent address. and there they'll scarcely find us (if they do, we'll move away still further: into now.'

[88] Noel Davis

[89] 'Supervision [remains] the signature pedagogy within the human services' according to Noble, Gray and Johnston, (2016) *Critical Supervision for the Human Services: A Social Model to Promote Learning and Value-based Practice*. London: Jessica Kingsley Publishers.

[90] In one of the earliest books to emerge in the field of supervision, Gerard Egan (1975) *The Skilled Helper: A Systematic Approach to Effective Helping*, Pacific Grove, California: Brooks Cole Publishing. Egan makes only one mention of supervision and it is to say this: 'a supervisor is someone who can tell you what you are doing right, so that you can keep on doing it and what you are doing wrong so that you can correct it.'(53) See also Alonso who writes: 'Supervisors serve as the keepers of the faith and the mentors of the young ... they teach, inspire, cajole and shape their students toward their own standard of professional excellence' cited in Michael Carroll (1996) *Counselling Supervision: Theory, Skills and Practice*, London: Cassell, 1.

[91] The seeds of cross-professional supervision were sown by Hawkins and Shohet in 1989 in their first edition of *Supervision in The Helping Professions* which was the first book on supervision to cross professional boundaries and suggest a generic model of supervision applicable to more than one context and one profession. But the heavy weight it paid to psychodynamic thinking in attending to the transferential aspects of the supervisory relationship (Eyes 3-6) left many thinking that, despite claims to the contrary, it betrayed more of a therapeutic than a cross professional paradigm. Two Irish supervisors, Bobby Moore (*Reflexive Supervision: A workbook for learning within and across professions,* 2017) and Ger Holton (unpublished doctoral thesis) have been the first to untether supervision from its therapeutic moorings and refashion it as truly cross professional.

About the Author

Dr Michael Paterson is a Scottish priest, psychotherapist, pastoral supervisor and Director of the Institute of Pastoral Supervision & Reflective Practice

He runs professional training in Pastoral Supervision in the UK, Malta and Australia and is a frequent conference speaker across the English speaking world.

His published works include

Pastoral Supervision: A Handbook (2nd edition 2015); Dutch edition 2019.

Enriching Ministry: Pastoral Supervision in Context (2014)

Childhood Sexual Abuse: Caring for Self and Others (2018)

Practical Theology in Progress: Showcasing an Emerging Discipline (2018).

Books in preparation include:

Creative Approaches in Pastoral Supervision

Pastoral Supervision in an Era of Change

A full list of publications and articles can be found at www.ipsrp.org.uk

PASTORAL: CONCERNING OR APPROPRIATE TO
THE GIVING OF SPIRITUAL GUIDANCE

SUPERVISION: SUPER = ABOVE, EXTRA
VISION = SEE, OBSERVE.

TRANSCEND
BE OR GO BEYOND THE RANGE OR
LIMITS OF (A FIELD OF ACTIVITY
OR CONCEPTUAL SPHERE)

TRANSFORMATIVE
CAUSING A MARKED CHANGE IN
SOMEONE OR SOMETHING

TRANSACTIONAL
RELATING TO EXCHANGE OR
INTERACTION BETWEEN PEOPLE

SUPERVISION PROCESS:
THE PURPOSE OF THE SUPERVISION
PROCESS IS TO PROVIDE A SAFE,
SUPPORTIVE OPPORTUNITY FOR
INDIVIDUALS TO ENGAGE IN
CRITICAL REFLECTION IN ORDER TO
RAISE ISSUES, EXPLORE PROBLEMS,
AND DISCOVER NEW WAYS OF
HANDLING BOTH THE SITUATION
AND ONESELF. A CRITICAL ASPECT
OF SUPERVISION LIES IN ITS
POTENTIAL TO EDUCATE.

About The Institute of Pastoral Supervision & Reflective Practice

The Institute of Pastoral Supervision & Reflective Practice is a community of practice specialising in Training, Research and Publishing in the field of Pastoral Supervision.

Associates are drawn from Scotland, Wales, England, Ireland, France and Australia.

Their specialisms include

Psychotherapy

Spiritual accompaniment

Missional planning

Local church leadership

Higher education

Doctoral supervision.

www.ipsrp.org.uk

Contact enquiries@ipsrp.org.uk

WHAT MOTIVATES
WHAT MATTERS
WHAT MEANING DO I GIVE
TRANSENDS ME, THE CLIENT
                    THE OUTCOME
                    THE CONTEXT
WHAT CONNECTS, WHAT DOESN'T
AM I OPEN TO DISCONNECTION.
WHAT RESONATES
WHAT FEELS CREATIVE, ENHANCING,
    ENABLING.
MEANING AND PURPOSE OF LIFE,
    WORK AND CONTEXT
DO I WANT TO BE MET
    "   "   TO MEET
DO I WANT TO LEARN
IS THIS A SAFE SPACE
AM I PROTECTING MY STATUS
    OR CONNECTING TO SHARE
RISK
RECIPROCATE
RUPTURE   RESONATE
REPAIR   REWARDING

BALANCE
BEING CLEAR ABOUT ROLES
BEING OPEN TO EXPLORE, HEAR
    " PREPARED TO CONNECT.

Printed in Great Britain
by Amazon

47830494R00095